TEACHING STRATEGIES THAT
Prepare Students
FOR
HIGH-STAKES
TESTS

TEACHING STRATEGIES THAT
Prepare Students
FOR
HIGH-STAKES
TESTS

DONNA WALKER TILESTON
SANDRA K. DARLING

CORWIN PRESS
A SAGE Company
Thousand Oaks, CA 91320

For information:

Corwin Press
A SAGE Company
2455 Teller Road
Thousand Oaks, California 91320
www.corwinpress.com

SAGE Ltd.
1 Oliver's Yard
55 City Road
London EC1Y 1SP
United Kingdom

SAGE India Pvt. Ltd.
B 1/I 1 Mohan Cooperative
    Industrial Area
Mathura Road, New Delhi 110 044
India

SAGE Asia-Pacific Pte. Ltd.
33 Pekin Street #02-01
Far East Square
Singapore 048763

Printed in the United States of America.

Library of Congress Cataloging-in-Publication Data

Tileston, Donna Walker.
Teaching strategies that prepare students for high-stakes tests/Donna Walker Tileston, Sandra K. Darling.
    p. cm.
Includes bibliographical references and index.
ISBN 978-1-4129-4975-0 (cloth)
ISBN 978-1-4129-4976-7 (pbk.)
    1. Educational tests and measurements—United States. 2. Education—Standards—United States. I. Darling, Sandra K. II. Title.

LB3051T563 2008
371.26—dc22   2008001235

This book is printed on acid-free paper.

08   09   10   11   12   10   9   8   7   6   5   4   3   2   1

Acquisitions Editor:	Carol Chambers Collins
Editorial Assistants:	Gem Rabanera, Brett Ory
Production Editor:	Cassandra Margaret Seibel
Copy Editor:	Jovey Stewart
Typesetter:	C&M Digitals (P) Ltd.
Proofreader:	Susan Schon
Indexer:	Judy Hunt
Cover Designer:	Lisa Riley

Contents

List of Figures

Acknowledgments

Corwin Press gratefully acknowledges the contributions of the following reviewers:

Betsy Carter
Director of Mathematics, K–12
Hamden Public Schools
Hamden, CT

Sandra Coelho
Associate Director for Mathematics, PIMMS
Wesleyan University
Middletown, CT

J-Petrina McCarty-Puhl
Science Teacher
Robert McQueen High School
Reno, NV

Phyllis Milne
Associate Director Curriculum and
    Student Achievement, and Adjunct Professor
George Washington University
York County School Division
Yorktown, VA

Patricia Palmer
Teacher
Wynford Schools
Bucyrus, OH

Laurie Peterman
Teacher
Andover High School
Andover, MN

About the Authors

Donna Walker Tileston has served education as a leader in teaching, administration, research, writing, software development, and national consulting for the past 30 years. She has been responsible for curriculum development, management, technology, finance, grants management, public relations, and drug abuse prevention programs. For the past 25 years she has been actively involved in brain research, including factors that inhibit learning or increase the brain's ability to put information into long-term memory. Tileston's 10-book collection *What Every Teacher Should Know* (Corwin Press, 2003) received the 2004 Distinguished Achievement Award for Excellence in Educational Publishing by the American Educational Publishers Association. Other Corwin Press titles include *Strategies for Active Learning* (2006); *What Every Parent Should Know About Schools, Standards, and High-Stakes Tests* (2005); *Training Manual for What Every Teacher Should Know* (2005); *Ten Best Teaching Practices: How Brain Research, Learning Styles and Standards Define Teaching Competencies* (2005); and *Strategies for Teaching Differently: On the Block or Not* (1998). Tileston has presented extensively at local, state, national, and international conferences, including in The Hague in November 2005 and in Prague during March 2006.

Sandra K. Darling is the founder and president of Learning Bridges. Grounded in five years of research, the Learning Bridges Aligned Instructional Database contains the most effective, research-based instructional strategies for the standards of all states—in rank order of their power to impact learning. Born into extreme poverty in rural Minnesota, Dr. Darling understands the power of having significant adults in her life who believed in her, held high expectations for her, and taught her the value of integrity. She received her bachelor's degree, three master's degrees, and a PhD from the University of Minnesota in related areas of education. She has coauthored three books in education and published articles in several education journals. She has presented to thousands of educators on standards-based education, curriculum alignment, inclusion practices, transformational leadership, school improvement, strategic planning, and assessment practices. She is the leading expert on aligning instructional strategies to content standards and delivering that instruction with the modifications to close the gap in achievement for diverse learners, that is, students from poverty, diverse cultures, and English language learners.

Introduction

I have known for some time that I wanted to write a book on standards and preparing for high-stakes testing. I had certainly written small bits on the subject in my book, *What Every Teacher Should Know About Assessment*, and in my book for parents, *What Every Parent Should Know About Standards and High-Stakes Testing*—both published by Corwin Press. Because there seems to be so much confusion over the role of standards and of "the test," I knew that I wanted to use the very best information available. My friend, Sandra Kay Darling, was my first choice in finding a collaborator on this project. Sandra Darling, along with her partner, Chuck Lowry, have created a database that aligns best practices to all 49 of the states' standards (Iowa uses the Iowa Test of Basic Skills) and ranks those instructional practices using their effect sizes. No longer do we need to "guess" which instructional practice to use to raise learning levels. We now know through a combination of brain research, studies of cultural differences, and meta-analysis results.

In this book, we have provided a model to help educators determine what benchmarks really require students to know and be able to do at given grade levels. With each chapter, we add to this model so that, by the conclusion of the book, educators have a framework for mapping daily lessons and assessments to state standards. The result should be higher test scores and greater student understanding of the learning. This is not a model for cramming for "the test," or even for teaching to the test. Rather, it is a model for teaching to standards and benchmarks and making formative assessment a part of the process. When we do that, state and national tests become less of a "gotcha."

Wiggins and McTighe (2005) stress that curriculum is first about the essential knowledge and skills; this body comprises the majority of what we should be teaching in school. What is nice to know and what individual communities want added to the curriculum comprise only a small part of what is taught and tested. If we truly are teaching to standards, then it follows that our lesson plans and our assessments will map to those standards and benchmarks. When we do this, state tests become just another step in the process. They should not be a surprise to students—but a culmination of all of the formative and summative assessments that have been going on in the classroom all along.

In one of the schools where we worked when we were first beginning to use some of these best practices, we found that we did not need to make a big deal about the state test—it was just more of the same kind of learning and assessing that had been going on before. As a matter of fact, our students told us that what they did on a daily basis was much more difficult than anything required on the state test. What's more, this was a high school that had previously been cited for its low test scores. In three years, this high school raised test scores by almost 30 percentile points. Now, we did many other things from changing the way that we taught to identified best practices to changing the way that we perceived the role of students. (Students became an integral part of the policies and procedures of the school). The point is that standards and benchmarks were a part of the day-to-day teaching and learning experience. They were also a part of the ongoing assessments in that school.

Chapter 1 introduces the reader to the first step in the mapping model, unpacking standards to examine the benchmarks or indicators. Readers will ask critical questions about what the benchmarks require students to know and be able to do. Chapter 1 will also examine the benchmarks to determine the level of complexity required of students.

In Chapter 2, we discuss the concept of types of knowledge contained in the standards (and on high-stakes tests) and why it is important to be able to identify which of the two types, declarative or procedural, are being required of students. Without this piece, standards and testing will not ever be achieved at a mastery level. Declarative and procedural knowledge are very different in terms of how they are taught and how they are assessed. The second step of the mapping model is introduced in this chapter as readers determine whether the benchmark requires declarative or procedural knowledge.

Chapter 3 moves the reader to an in-depth look at declarative knowledge in terms of how it should be taught and assessed. Throughout this chapter, we discuss how to identify declarative knowledge in the standards, and the best instructional practices for teaching that knowledge. Declarative knowledge is stored in the semantic pathway of the brain. This pathway is not very reliable when it comes to retrieval. Unless the information stored has a hook or pattern through which the student can recall the information, it is often just "in there someplace—but we can't remember it." We have all had the experience of needing information from our memory pathways and not being able to recall it. Kids will often say, "I know I know that, I just can't remember." Add to that the many English language learners in today's classrooms and you have a double whammy. They have tried to store information in an area that is not very reliable even to students with good vocabulary skills, and they don't have the vocabulary themselves to be able to retrieve it. We show you how to teach vocabulary in such a way that students remember it for life—not just for the test. Readers will be provided with the impact on learning for several best practices that address declarative knowledge.

Chapter 4 deals with the other type of knowledge: procedural knowledge. This is the type of knowledge that involves processes, of doing something with the declarative knowledge. In this chapter, we discuss how to identify this type of knowledge and how to teach it to students in a way that is meaningful. All of the strategies in this book have a high effect on student learning; this is one of the definitions of "best practices." By this chapter of the book, readers will have moved the mapping model to a fairly complex level. They will identify critical benchmarks, decide whether they are declarative or procedural in nature and at what level students will be expected to know and use the benchmark. In addition, the reader will have solutions for teaching these benchmarks based on the review of more than 32,000 studies.

In Chapter 5, we have provided the reader with a method for mapping classroom lessons and units to the state benchmarks and standards. We wanted to provide a manageable method for aligning instructional practices and day-to-day assessments to state standards. No more guessing what is the best way to teach to standards; we have the proof from research on which instructional strategies will make the most difference in student learning.

This book was written to provide scaffolding for teachers, to empower them so that they can experience greater success in the classroom and to break down barriers that are keeping students from demonstrating mastery of the standards.

Zooming In on the Standards

Americans expect strict standards to govern construction of buildings, bridges, highways, and tunnels—shoddy work would put lives at risk. They expect stringent standards to protect their drinking water, the food they eat, the air they breathe . . . Standards are created because they improve the activity of life. (p. 8)

—Diane Ravitch, *National Standards in American Education* (1995)

Visit any school these days and you will surely hear teachers discussing "the test." Pressure has never been higher to make sure that students show mastery on state assessment tests. In fact, many states reward teachers and administrators for bringing up the test scores of their students and often dole out funding based on student success. States are also denying increases on the salary schedule as a punishment based on student test results. Merit pay based on student performance is a hot topic nationally.

Society and government entities require that we measure quality in education and that we measure our progress against a set of standards. Many books on the market explain the *standards movement* or theories behind the standards. That is not the purpose of this book. This book is written to help educators determine the next steps. That is, how can we seamlessly integrate standards into the classroom so that state tests become merely another form of summative assessment of the knowledge and processes learned? Also, how can we determine exactly what students are expected to know and should be able to do at each grade level?

We were a little nervous when it came time for the state test in the first school in which we integrated these ideas. We had not taught "to the test"; instead, we had taught to standards and we had measured progress as we taught. This was the first challenge to see if our research and beliefs would hold up about just teaching to standards and applying formative assessment along the way. What if the research failed?

So we gave the students a little pep talk before the state test much as educators all over the country do on test day. After the test was over, several of our students came to us and said, "What is the big deal about the test? It is just what we do every day—only what we do daily is harder!"

That is exactly where we want to be in terms of high stakes testing—just another measurement of what we do on a daily basis.

THE FORGOTTEN PART OF THE TRIANGLE

Figure 1.1 is an example of the type of graph we often see when talking about alignment of the curriculum. Educators often say that if the curriculum is aligned, we will have a set of standards that are written, that we will teach to those standards, and then we will assess those standards. It sounds so simple; then why all the controversy?

This country has spent countless dollars on aligning state assessments to standards. Testing companies pore over test questions to be sure that they really do test what the standards say will be tested. They work with state education departments to be sure that there are no "gotchas." The assumption seems to be if a set of standards were written and disseminated, and if state tests were designed to assess whether those standards were mastered by students, then teachers would automatically know the best practices for teaching those standards.

This is where the model breaks down: Teachers were not given enough scaffolding. There was not enough research-based information about what really works with kids regarding the specific types of knowledge needed to ensure their success. The differentiation between various cultures, poverty, and English language learners was

Figure 1.1 Alignment of the curriculum

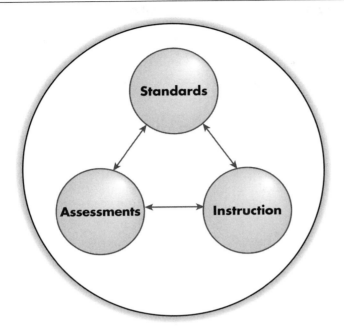

not provided to the people who needed to know it the most: the teachers. In this book, we will provide educators not only with the "how to" but with scientific evidence on which instructional practices make the most difference in student learning.

Our scientific evidence is based on a review of more than 32,000 studies housed in a data-bank owned by Sandra Darling's company, Learning Bridges. In this book, you will get a peek at some of those studies and what they say about instructional strategies that really do make the most difference in student learning. If you are new to meta-analysis, here is a brief summary of what we mean when we talk about effect sizes.

META-ANALYSIS

We have all been in training sessions where a presenter says, "I know this works because it works in my school." We would then all run out and try it in our schools only to be dismayed that we did not get the same results; we may even have gotten negative results. What happened? One study is not enough to be considered quality research. Rather, we have come to look at studies of many studies. We have also begun to look at other factors such as the demographics of the groups studied and whether the results were sustained over time.

Meta-analysis is a study of many studies on a given instructional practice. Fortunately for us as educators who may have been out of statistics classes for a while, effect sizes can be mathematically translated into percentiles. Throughout this book we will provide instructional strategies along with the effect size translated into percentiles. That means if the instructional practice is used correctly in the classroom, this is the effect that you can expect for your students' learning. For example, Figure 1.2 illustrates that an effect size translated into a 30 percentile gain means that if the instructional practice is used correctly in the classroom, teachers can expect that the average score on an assessment will move forward by 30 percentile points.

Figure 1.2   Using bell curve to show 30 percentile gain

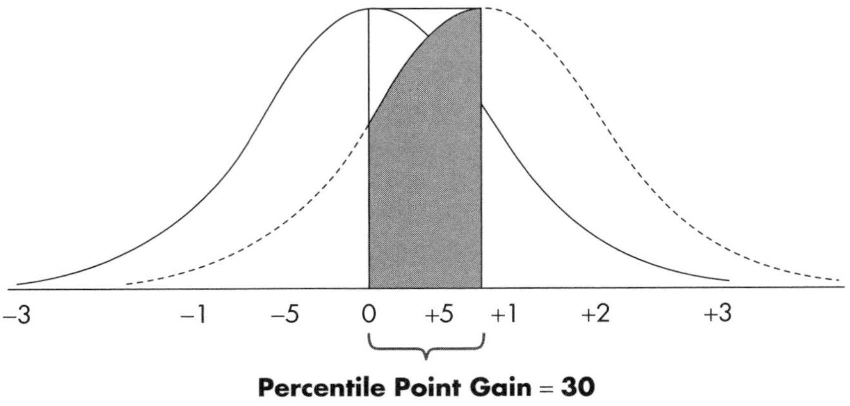

Percentile Point Gain = 30

BREAKING DOWN STANDARDS INTO MANAGEABLE PARTS

A *content standard* is defined as "a description of what students should know and be able to do within a particular discipline" (Kendall, Ryan, & Richardson, 2005, p. 1). Content standards were deliberately written in broad terms so that educators could determine the appropriate level(s) for teaching and testing based on their student populations, local curriculum, and other factors. For example, a content standard might be written like these four standards for English Language Arts available from the New York State Education Department Web site:

Standard I: Language for information and understanding

Standard II: Language for literary response and expression

Standard III: Language for critical analysis and evaluation

Standard IV: Language for social interaction

According to Kendall, Ryan, and Richardson, other terms used by states for content standards include "goals," "expectations," and "learning results."

This same content standard would be found for all grade levels from K–12. Therefore the content standard alone is not a good identifier of what students need to know and be able to do at a given grade level.

The number of content standards varies from state to state, with some states having as few as five and others with so many, it would be difficult to teach them all. Standards are general in nature, written as strands that go across the grade levels and have vertical alignment. Vertical alignment of standards assures that prerequisite skills for a specific set of grade-level standards are taught in the preceding grade levels. In other words, the prerequisite skills for 6th grade geometry are stated as learning expectations (grade-level standards) in grades K–5.

When a content standard is too broad-based to be used for lesson planning and assessment in the classroom, it is divided into strands or topics. For example, the content standards for New York for English Language Arts are broken down into substandards of listening and reading or speaking and writing. Each substandard also lists a *key idea* to help the reader determine the emphasis of the standard. For example:

Standard IV: Language for social interaction (the general standard found at all grade levels)

Speaking and writing (substandard)

Written communication for social interaction requires using written messages to establish, maintain, and enhance personal relationships with others. (This is the *key idea*.)

Seven to thirteen performance indicators (or benchmarks) follow next, such as

1. Students produce oral and written reports on topics related to all school subjects. (Example of a performance indicator or benchmark)

If all we had were the general standards statements, as educators we would be scratching our heads to determine what our students really need to know and be able to do. Broad content statements do not provide enough detail to inform instruction. As a result, what educators would expect students to learn would depend on individual teacher interpretation. In the absence of clear learning expectations, we would become a nation of schools and classrooms that would be guided by textbooks and the individuals who teach in the classroom. Students who move from school to school (even within the same school system) might not have any consistency in what was taught at that subject or grade level. Equity would be a major concern and justifiably so.

Fortunately, it is not the standards alone that guide us on what our students need to know and be able to do. It is, rather, the grade-level benchmarks or performance indicators that guide instruction and also state testing. Benchmarks (some states call them indicators) tell us how the standard is interpreted for given grade levels. A grade-level benchmark is a clear, specific description of the knowledge or skill that students should acquire by a particular point in their schooling.

According to Squires (2004), a benchmark should not be so narrow that it could be mastered in an afternoon and not so broad that it might take several months of instruction. In addition, it must be specific enough to inform instruction. Teachers need to have enough information to identify an instructional approach, methodology, appropriate means for assessing student learning, and instructional resources in order to design their units of instruction and lessons from the grade-level benchmarks.

Benchmarks enable an educator to determine what students at a particular grade level should know and be able to do in order to show mastery of the standard. Because of vertical alignment in grade-level benchmarks, teachers can be assured that the prerequisite knowledge and skills are introduced, taught, and mastered in earlier grade levels. Grade-level benchmarks also identify where specific knowledge and skills are introduced, where they are reinforced, and where they will be tested through formative and summative assessments to determine that students have mastered the benchmark.

Questions answered by benchmarks or indicators include

1. What will students at a specific grade level need to know about the standard?

2. What will students at a specific grade level need to be able to do with the knowledge?

3. What level of understanding will students at any given grade level be expected to achieve?

Let's look closer at these three essential questions to determine what is important for us to know in order to effectively use standards in the classroom.

What Will Students Need to Know About the Standard?

Understanding what students will need to know in order to show mastery on state tests is not a mystery. The authors of the standards in each state have spent countless hours providing that information within the benchmarks or indicators. Indeed, testing companies use this information as their guide in writing test questions. Before testing companies approve test questions for final editing, they match the questions with the benchmark or indicator being tested and they look carefully to be sure they are testing exactly what they say is being tested. For example:

Geometric shapes: Students will recognize and use geometric shapes (the standard).

Grade 1 (benchmark): Students will recognize a *circle, square, triangle, cube, sphere,* and *rectangle* in real world situations.

As educators, we recognize from this benchmark or indicator that students will need to know a circle, a square, a triangle, a cube, a sphere, and a rectangle. They will not just need to know the definitions but they must *recognize* them. If students recognize a sphere, for example, then they know the characteristics of a sphere; they know why an object is a sphere rather than a square or a cube. To ensure that students can recognize these shapes, it is important to teach the vocabulary words: circle, square, triangle, cube, sphere and rectangle, and also include the attributes of each of these shapes.

What Will Students Need to Be Able to Do With the Knowledge?

Let's look again at the benchmark:

Grade 1: Students will *recognize* a circle, square, triangle, cube, sphere, and rectangle *in real world situations.*

What does this benchmark say about what students will need to be able to do with a circle, square, triangle, cube, sphere, and rectangle? It says that students will recognize them in real world situations.

Benchmarks often include "real world situations" as a part of the expectation. We see this more often in higher grade levels. Specifically, benchmarks tell us that, while students might be able to demonstrate understanding of the concept in a classroom setting, they must also be able to transfer that knowledge to the real world outside the classroom. For example, a student might be able to perform math solutions using slope in classroom paper and pencil problems, but can that student apply the knowledge to real world uses of slope? This says that students will not only have to recognize the shapes but recognize them in objects in the real world: i.e., will they recognize a picture frame in the shape of a square, a slice of cheese as a triangle, a bicycle wheel as a circle, or a globe as being a sphere?

An assessment question on a state test might show a picture of a globe and ask students to circle the correct shape from a list of four possibilities such as circle, cube, sphere, and square.

This is a legitimate question because it asks students to recognize one of the given shapes from the benchmark list in a real world context. If the test had asked students to identify a real world object in the shape of a cone, this would not be an appropriate question for this benchmark because educators and students were not told they had to recognize a cone. Benchmarks or indicators help to prevent surprises or "gotchas" in the summative assessment itself.

At What Level Will Students Be Expected to Achieve?

As we look at products of the learning process, we will also look at their level of complexity. Bloom's *Taxonomy* (1956) is the best resource out there to perform this job. In the schools that we work with, we recommend that this taxonomy is taught to all students from elementary through high school and that the terminology be used in all classrooms. Students need to be aware of their own level of learning and its degree of complexity. For our mapping purposes, we will use this taxonomy and the following definitions. The definitions come from *What Every Teacher Should Know About Special Learners* (Tileston, 2003). (Used with permission.)

1. **Knowledge**—O'Tuel and Bullard (1993) describe the knowledge level as "what one can remember from previous learning or experience. It involves simple recall and recognition; the learner may have acquired the information by rote learning" (p. 19).

   An example of a question from the knowledge level might be, "What is a noun?" Verbs that reflect this level of understanding include

List	Define
Describe	Label
Identify	Recall
State	

   At this level, students do not need to understand the information, just be able to repeat it. For example, a student might memorize that 4×4 equals 16 but not truly understand the concept of why $4 \times 4 = 16$. A student might create a timeline but not understand the significance or the information contained within the timeline. At this level, students simply know facts which they can write down or verbalize as they were taught in the classroom. Real world application is not expected at this level.

2. **Comprehension**—Comprehension occurs when students show some degree of understanding of the information from the knowledge level. For example, at the knowledge level, students might make a timeline of the events that led to World War II, but that does not mean they understand the information. They would need to tell why the events led to World War II to be working at the comprehension level. Being able to explain a math problem to another person is an example of demonstrating comprehension.

Verbs that we associate with comprehension include

Paraphrase	Report
Explain	Review
Group	Describe
Conclude	Translate
Restate	Give examples

At this level, students not only know the information, they understand it. They comprehend how $4 \times 4 = 16$ and can demonstrate the concept. The learning has personal meaning to them at this point.

3. **Application**—The application level marks the beginning of higher-level thinking. At this level, the student knows the information (knowledge), has some understanding of it (comprehension), and can use the information in a situation other than the one in which it was first learned.

Some verbs for the application level include

Compute	Dramatize
Organize	Illustrate
Apply	Sketch
Summarize	Solve
Classify	Apply
Construct	Operate
Translate	Use

At this level, students know that $4 \times 4 = 16$; they can demonstrate the concept, and they can use the concept in classroom and real world situations. Our first graders who can identify shapes in the real world are working at this level.

4. **Analysis**—At the analysis level, students can break information apart, analyze it, compare it, and look at the organizational

sets. The compare and contrast organizer that you will learn in Chapter 4 is an example of using analysis.

Some verbs that we identify with analysis are as follows:

Take apart	Pattern
Fill in	Analyze
Take away	Calculate
Combine	Experiment
Differentiate	Test
Divide	Compare and
Isolate	contrast
Order	Diagram
Distinguish	Debate
Dissect	Question
Relate	Solve

At this level students can break down the knowledge into component parts. Breaking down the standards and benchmarks so that we can analyze what is required is an example of working at this level.

5. **Synthesis**—Synthesis involves creativity and the ability to see things in new ways. O'Tuel and Bullard (1993) say that synthesis "includes the ability to organize, to arrange elements in meaningful relationships, and to make inferences about those relationships" (p. 20).

When students write compositions, regardless of the type, they are creating something new based on what they know. Much of the synthesis relies on the work of analysis.

Some verbs used in synthesis include

Compose	Regroup
Add to	Systematize
Predict	Symbolize
Translate	Create
Extend	Formulate
Hypothesize	Modify
Design	Minimize
Reconstruct	Connect
Reorganize	Set up

Generate   Design

Plan   Create

Students who can synthesize can take something apart and put it back together in new and/or unique ways. This book is an attempt to synthesize high-stakes testing so that educators will have a model to improve students' demonstration of understanding.

6. **Evaluation**—Evaluation is often considered to be the most complex part of the taxonomy. It requires the ability to make judgments. An example of evaluation might be, "After studying the information on genomes and transplants, discuss your ideas about the ethics of transplanting embryonic tissue to save lives." At the elementary level, you might ask, "Was the argument provided in the poem, 'Earrings,' by Judith Viorst valid? Defend your decision. Tell why you think it was or was not a good argument."

Verbs used with this level of thinking include the following:

Defend   Value

Interpret   Assess

Verify   Judge

Conclude   Debate

Appraise   Justify

Rate   Evaluate

Students who can evaluate can make judgments based on evidence, on the ability to empathize, and on being able to see from many perspectives. Students asked to write a letter to the editor on a given topic are being assessed on their ability to evaluate.

Throughout this book we will examine assessments in terms of the required depth of knowledge.

IN SUMMARY

State standards are written in broad terms and are aligned vertically throughout the subject area and grade levels. Students will know that geometric terms are a typical standard found in grades K–12. Standards alone, however, are not enough to make decisions about what to teach and assess. Benchmarks (called performance indicators in some states) determine what students should know and be able to do at each grade level. When we break down the benchmarks, we find three kinds of information:

1. *What students need to know in order to show mastery.* In the early days of television, a popular police drama made a saying famous by its repetitive use by one of the show's main characters, Sergeant Friday: "Just the facts, ma'am, just the facts." This is a good analogy for declarative knowledge.

2. *What students need to be able to do with factual information in order to demonstrate their understanding.* We call this procedural knowledge. Procedural knowledge should be taught and assessed differently from knowledge. Brain research indicates that procedural knowledge is stored and retrieved in a different part of the brain than declarative knowledge.

3. *The level of understanding expected of students to demonstrate their learning at a particular grade level.* Most states use Bloom's *Taxonomy* as a guide in determining the depth of understanding.

It is important to identify this information so that we can make informed decisions about which instructional practices will make the most difference in student learning.

Figure 1.3   Step 1 of the model

Standard I: Geometric Principles

Students will understand basic and advanced principles of geometry.

Benchmark	Level of Understanding K=knowledge C=comprehension Ap=application An=analysis S=synthesis E=evaluation
Knows basic geometric language for describing and naming shapes (e.g., square, triangle, cube, circle, sphere)	K
Understands the basic properties and similarities and differences in shapes	An

Figure 1.3 provides a graphic organizer to assist educators as they analyze the benchmarks. Step 1 involves charting the benchmarks or indicators under each standard (by grade level and subject area). Next, identify the level of taxonomy that Bloom's students are asked to demonstrate. This step will help to identify the level of understanding you can expect from your students as they enter your grade level or subject area. It also is a guide for educators who teach to determine the level of understanding that we should expect from our students.

2

Identifying the Types of Knowledge

B enchmarks within the standards require students to respond to two types of knowledge: declarative and procedural. We know from brain research that these two types of knowledge should be taught differently because they are assessed differently.

In this chapter, we will look at the benchmarks to see where to find the two types of knowledge requirements and the steps to teaching each.

USING BENCHMARKS TO IDENTIFY TESTED CONTENT

What students will need to know and be able to do is embedded within the benchmarks. Taking a state exam should not be reason for weeping and gnashing of teeth. If lessons are based on standards and benchmarks and day-to-day assessments—both formative and summative—then the state test should just be an end-of-course test. What is expected to be learned (benchmarks) is what should be taught (instruction) in the classroom. Classroom assessments and formative tests that measure student learning of the benchmarks will *predict* the results on the state test.

UNPACKING THE STANDARDS AND BENCHMARKS

According to Kendall, Ryan, and Richardson (2005), "unpacking the standards" is a phrase "commonly used to describe the analytic process of identifying the knowledge and/or skills that make up a benchmark. Like the benchmark, the knowledge or skill statement is written as either declarative or procedural knowledge" (p. 2).

The first step in determining instruction and classroom assessment is unpacking the standards and benchmarks in order to determine whether it represents declarative or procedural knowledge. We need to know this because

1. We *teach* to each type of knowledge differently, and

2. We *assess* each type of knowledge differently.

How, then, do you know which type of knowledge (declarative or procedural) is required of students in your state benchmarks? Below we provide a list of questions to ask as you read your benchmarks. These questions will help you determine the type of knowledge your state requires. Then you can make more informed decisions about how best to teach those benchmarks.

---

1. Does the standard contain generalizations, principles, or overarching ideas, and/or what examples will be used to support these?

    Yes = Declarative

    No = Procedural

2. Does the standard contain essential time sequences, cause/effect sequences, or episodes that students will need to remember and use at a later date?

    Yes = Declarative

    No = Procedural

3. Does the standard contain essential vocabulary terms or phrases that would be important for students to learn?

    Yes = Declarative

    No = Procedural

4. Does the standard contain any processes that students will need to practice, and what are the subcomponents of these processes?

    Yes = Procedural

    No = Declarative

5. Does the standard contain any skills (tactics or algorithms) that students will need to practice in order to gain proficiency, and what are the steps or rules that students will need for these skills?

> Yes = Procedural
>
> No = Declarative

6. Does measurement of the standard require the use of explicit examples, relationships, and the absence of misconceptions (in those examples)?

> Yes = Declarative
>
> No = Procedural

7. Does measurement of the standard require a performance that is carried out with ease, a level of automaticity, and without error?

> Yes = Procedural
>
> No = Declarative

8. If critical attributes of both declarative and procedural knowledge are contained in the standard, categorize it as *both*.

SOURCE: Alignment of Instruction to Content (Patent Pending) by Sandra Darling. Reprinted with permission.

For the sample benchmarks below, use the questions above to check for your own understanding between declarative and procedural benchmarks.

The student will

1. Understand the distinguishing characteristics of a variety of literary genres (e.g., fiction, nonfiction, fantasy, fable, etc.) Declarative, procedural, or both?

   This benchmark (found in some form in every state's benchmarks) is *declarative* in nature because it requires that students know a list of vocabulary words (the literary genres) and that they know what makes the definitions unique. For example, why is a fantasy a fantasy instead of a fable?

2. Write fluently for a variety of occasions, audiences, and purposes, making appropriate choices regarding style, tone, level of detail, and organization. Declarative, procedural, or both?

   This benchmark is *procedural* because it requires students to demonstrate understanding by writing and using the heuristics of style tone and so on.

3. Recognize the use of specific literary devices (e.g., foreshadowing, flashback, progressive and digressive time, suspense, figurative language, description, metaphor). Declarative, procedural, or both?

    When the verb "recognize" is used, the benchmark is *declarative* in nature. Students will need to know the vocabulary words, foreshadowing, flashback, progressive and digressive time, suspense, figurative language, description, and metaphor.

4. Understand the properties (e.g., relative magnitude, density, absolute value) of the real number system and its subsystems (e.g., irrational numbers, natural numbers, integers, rational numbers). Declarative, procedural, or both?

    Declarative—Students know and understand the critical attributes of the properties and subsystems which is information.

5. Solves linear equations using concrete, informal, and formal methods (e.g., using properties graphing ordered pairs, using slope-intercept form. Declarative, procedural, or both?

    This *procedural* benchmark requires that students *demonstrate* they can solve linear equations using various methods.

6. Uses specific strategies (e.g., front-end estimation, rounding) to estimate computations and to check the reasonableness of computational results. Declarative, procedural, or both?

    This benchmark represents *procedural* knowledge as students must *demonstrate* the use of specific strategies to check for reasonableness.

Once we know how to examine our state's grade level benchmarks to determine the type of knowledge represented in them, the next step is identifying how we teach and assess to each type of knowledge.

DECLARATIVE KNOWLEDGE STRATEGY: TEACHING VOCABULARY

One of the most powerful and "broad brushes" for teaching declarative benchmarks is appropriately teaching the vocabulary of the benchmark. Approximately 80 to 90 percent of any given state test is based on the vocabulary and concepts of the standards (Marzano & Kendall, 1996). As a matter of fact, in schools where teachers are taught how to appropriately teach vocabulary of the standards by both McREL (Mid-continent Research for Education & Learning) and Learning Bridges, the average test score increased as much as

20 percentile points. Think about it, would it be helpful in your school if you could raise the average test score by 20 percentile points? How do we find this vocabulary that is essential to mastering the benchmarks? Examine the sample benchmarks below. Can you identify which vocabulary or concept words that students would need to know in order to show mastery? The student will

Example 1: Understand the organizational patterns of informational texts (e.g., chronological, logical, and sequential orders; compare and contrast; cause and effect; proposition and support)

Vocabulary terms for Example 1:

Cause and effect	Organizational pattern
Chronological order	Posing and answering questions
Classification and division	
Compare and contrast	Problem and solution
Hierarchical relationships	Proposition and support
Informational text	Sequential order
Logical order	Spatial order

Is the vocabulary coming from the benchmark language itself? Is the vocabulary derived from prerequisite knowledge? Is the vocabulary coming from terms required for instruction? If you answered "yes" to all of these questions, you are correct.

Whenever we train teachers on critical content, we always say, "Teach the vocabulary first!" How could students understand the content and participate in the learning from instruction if they did not know the vocabulary of the subject? Marzano, Pickering, and Pollock (2001) reinforce this by reminding us that knowledge of a subject is related directly to understanding the vocabulary associated with that subject. Every subject has its own vocabulary. Science includes words like phylum; social studies have words like civilizations; and mathematics has terms like function. In mathematics, if the teacher says, "Your weight is a function of your height," and you don't know what *function* means, then you are going to have difficulty making sense out of what the teacher says. You are going to go home with homework that makes no sense to you. On the other hand, if the teacher has taught the vocabulary of the lesson first, you will know that *function* is a relationship between two things like height and weight. As one goes up, the other goes up. Isn't it generally true that as you have grown in height over the years, your weight has gone up as well? We never take it for granted that our students know the vocabulary; we teach vocabulary first and we find out if they understand it. In Chapter 3 we will discuss how to effectively teach vocabulary—not just for the state test, but for life.

PROCEDURAL KNOWLEDGE BENCHMARKS

You may be thinking, "Wait, the state assessments are not simply vocabulary tests" and you are right. State assessments make the assumption that students know the vocabulary of the benchmarks. Procedural knowledge comprises the processes, skills, tactics, and algorithms they will need to use in order to demonstrate application of declarative knowledge. Again, understanding the distinction between declarative and procedural knowledge in grade-level benchmarks is critical for the following reasons:

1. The brain processes, stores, and retrieves procedural information and declarative information differently.

2. Declarative and procedural information should be taught differently.

3. Declarative and procedural knowledge are assessed differently.

4. Declarative and procedural learning require different levels of motivation.

5. Declarative and procedural knowledge require different prerequisites. For example, declarative knowledge requires that students have language acquisition skills to respond to learning, to store it, and to be able to retrieve it when they want to use it in some way. This explains, in part, why English language learners struggle with tests based on vocabulary.

6. Declarative knowledge is generally a prerequisite for procedural knowledge in learning since skills, processes, tactics, and algorithms require the information—declarative knowledge—in order to perform (procedural) a process or skill.

Here's an example from our own background that distinguishes the two forms of knowledge and how we prepared and received our license to drive a car.

We first obtained a book of the rules of the road (e.g., drive on the right, don't cross double lines, etc.), the names (vocabulary) of the parts of the car about which we should pay attention (e.g., brake pedal, shift selector, speedometer), the names of road indicators (e.g., gore point, no-passing sign, merging lane, etc.). Then we took a test (usually a multiple-choice test) on the *declarative knowledge* about driving. We could now communicate because we had the terms. Did we get our license to drive yet? No, there was that other part! We now had to get behind the wheel. We practiced, and we developed skills in parallel parking, passing, stopping, and for some of us...not killing the engine when using a clutch. When we thought we had reached a sufficient degree of proficiency, we took a different kind of test that required us to demonstrate our skills (procedural knowledge) in driving a car. If we had passed both the multiple-choice test (of declarative knowledge) and the behind-the-wheel test (of procedural knowledge), then, and only then, did we get our license to drive a car.

PROCEDURAL KNOWLEDGE STRATEGY: HEURISTICS

A powerful strategy and "broad brush" for teaching procedural grade-level benchmarks is called *heuristics.* It can increase learning as much as 38 percentile points (Darling, 1999). What are heuristics? Heuristics are the general rules, tactics, and strategies, as opposed to a set of rigid steps, for implementing processes such as decision making, experimental inquiry, problem solving, investigating, reading, speaking, and listening. Students apply and practice the general rules, tactics, and strategies with attention to how they might be improved (Marzano, 1998). When teachers provide students with a guide that outlines the components and subcomponents of a process, they are providing students with a heuristic. In Chapter 4 we will examine some heuristics for teaching skills, processes, and other procedural benchmarks so students become confident in their ability to demonstrate their learning.

IN SUMMARY

State tests are based on declarative and procedural knowledge. According to Marzano and Kendall (2006), about 80 to 90 percent of the success on any state test is based on *declarative* knowledge—primarily knowing the vocabulary of the standards. What students do with that vocabulary, i.e., how they demonstrate proficiency with skills, processes, algorithms, and procedures, is called *procedural* knowledge. When we analyze the standards and benchmarks to determine which vocabulary is necessary to understand the subject area and then isolate the processes that will be required of students, we call this *unpacking the standards.*

In the chapters that follow, we will *unpack the standards* and will discuss how to effectively teach and appropriately assess both declarative and procedural knowledge benchmarks for student success on the standards-based assessment—state or local.

Figure 2.1 is a graphic organizer that provides the second step in the model for preparing for high-stakes testing.

Figure 2.1   Standards model: Step 2

Standard I: Geometric Principles

Students will understand basic and advanced principles of geometry.

Benchmark	Type of Knowledge D=Declarative P=Procedural B=Both	Level of Understanding K=Knowledge C=Comprehension Ap=Application An=Analysis S=Synthesis E=Evaluation	Essential Vocabulary
Knows basic geometric language for describing and naming shapes (e.g., square, triangle, cube, circle, sphere)	D	K	Shapes Square Triangle Cube Circle Sphere

Understands the basic properties and similarities and differences in shapes	D	An	Similarity
			Difference
			Properties
			  • Corner
			  • Round
			  • Point
			  • Two or three dimensionality
			  • Symmetry

3

Teaching and Assessing Declarative Knowledge Standards

We educators stand at a special point in time. This is not because a new decade, century, and millennium have begun (although this phenomenon certainly brings new opportunities and complexities). Rather, it is because the "art" of teaching is rapidly becoming the "science" of teaching, and this is a relatively new phenomenon. (p. 1)

—Robert Marzano,
Debra Pickering, and Jane Pollock,
Classroom Instruction That Works (2001)

In Chapter 2, we discussed how to identify and isolate declarative information in the standards. Using the graphic organizer, benchmarks were identified as either requiring declarative (D), procedural (P), or both kinds of knowledge (B). We said that this is an important step because it guides us as we look for the most effective ways to teach our students. Declarative information is usually stored in the semantic memory system—the least reliable of the three memory systems. In order to retrieve information stored in the semantic memory system, students must have a connector to the information. English language learners who do not have the language acquisition skills to store and retrieve declarative information appropriately will struggle with recall. This may, in fact, account for the overall test scores of English language learners which seem to be lower than their English-speaking counterparts. If about 85 percent of any given state assessment is based on declarative knowledge (Marzano & Kendall, 1996), then it stands to reason that English language learners will struggle.

We know from the research that many of our students from poverty come to us with fewer vocabulary words than their fellow students from middle and upper economic status. These students also tend to do poorer on state assessments.

In this chapter, we will discuss how to teach declarative knowledge in the classroom and to tie that teaching to the declarative knowledge contained in the benchmarks. Let's take a closer look at declarative knowledge and the classroom.

DECLARATIVE KNOWLEDGE

Declarative knowledge involves knowing the "what" or "what it is." It is learned information rather than learned procedures and usually involves components or parts. It could be information or terminology about a concept or topic. Declarative knowledge might mean being able to remember a list of steps, such as division steps (i.e., divide, multiply, subtract, bring down); facts, such as multiplication facts; concepts, such as civil rights; vocabulary definitions, principles, ideas, understandings, and generalizations. In our daily assessments of declarative knowledge, we need to make sure that our assessments only assess the "what" rather than the application of that knowledge (Doty, 2007).

Specific examples of declarative knowledge include

- Understands the concept of "freedom of speech"
- Knows the answer to 2×5
- Understands the properties and theorems of roots, exponents, and logarithms

- Understands that words and pictures convey ideas or meaning in a text
- Understands that animals have characteristics that help them adapt to their environment
- Knows the causes and effects of the American Revolution
- Knows the rules that govern various sports
- Understands the concept of "conservation"
- Identifies even and odd numbers on a number line

Note the passive verbs *know, identify,* and *understand* (above) that demonstrate to us that the standards are declarative in nature.

Teachers can assess this type of knowledge in the classroom by asking students to provide examples and to identify relationships and distinctions. Appropriate classroom testing formats to assess declarative knowledge might include

- Completing a cause and effect chart, such as a fishbone. In Figure 3.1 students are given the effect (World War II). They must complete the fishbone by writing in causes on each of the fishbones. The fishbones could be further defined as causes related to World War I, causes related to individual governments, causes related to the world economy, and so on.

Figure 3.1   Fishbone example

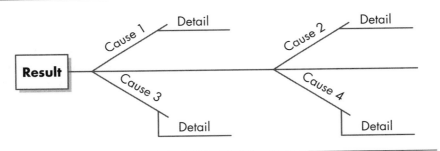

- Labeling examples and nonexamples of a concept or idea. A teacher introducing symmetry might want to show students visual examples of symmetry and examples of what symmetry is not.
- Completing a "selected response" test (i.e., matching, multiple choice, true/false). Although we strongly believe that once we begin to use ongoing methods for assessing and the need for end-of-unit tests lessen, there will be times when a paper and pencil test is needed. Selected response tests are effective if the test is well written. Fisher and Frey (2007) provide a wonderful checklist in their book, *Checking for Understanding,* that is a great guide for putting together good tests. For example, they

suggest asking the following questions if writing a test with matching items:

○ Is the material for the two lists homogeneous?

○ Is the list of responses longer or shorter than the list of premises?

○ Are the responses brief and on the right-hand side?

○ Have the responses been placed in alphabetical or numerical order?

○ Do the directions indicate the basis for matching?

○ Do the directions indicate how many times each response may be used?

○ Are all of the matching items on the same page (Fisher & Frey, 2007, p.104–105)?

• Completing or creating a graphic representation that demonstrates understanding of the objective. A *mind map* is a great way to do this. A good mind map will follow these heuristics:

○ Center circle contains the topic.

○ Each spoke coming from the center circle to the component part or idea should be in a different color. If we ask students to create a mind map in small groups using chart paper, we ask each student to draw with a different color marker so that we know all students are participating. The reason for using a different color for each sub-topic or idea is to give a context (or hook) to the brain.

○ Use words and pictures. We use pictures because it gives context to the information for brain processing and because 87 percent (Jensen, 2003) of the students in any given classroom are visual or visual/kinesthetic learners. On those days when they are trying to recall the information, they will more likely recall the picture first and then the words.

○ Figure 3.2 shows an example of a mind map for nouns. Unfortunately, the print world makes it prohibitive for us to show you a mind map in color.

THE PROCESS OF TEACHING DECLARATIVE KNOWLEDGE

Declarative knowledge refers to all of the things we want our students to know as a result of the lessons. For example, when teaching a unit on parts of speech, it's important for the students to know the vocabulary associated with parts of speech, along with the rules involved in using parts of speech in both written and spoken language. In order for the students to meet these goals, a series of processes take place in the brain. The following briefly explains those processes.

Figure 3.2   Mind maps for nouns and pronouns

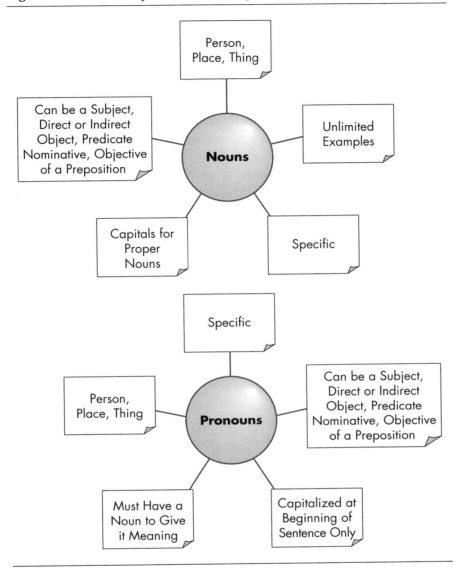

Constructing Meaning

The brain naturally looks for patterns in order to find meaning from new learning. As a matter of fact, the background knowledge of our students is essential to their ability to construct meaning from declarative information. Marzano (2004) notes:

> Although it is true that the extent to which students will learn this new content is dependent on factors such as the skill of the teacher, the interest of the student, and the complexity of the content, the research literature supports one compelling fact: what students *already know* about the content is one of

the strongest indicators of how well they will learn new information relative to the content. (p. 1)

The following ideas from Tileston (2003) provide ways that educators can help students construct meaning from the learning:

- Create patterns and connections between what the learner already knows and the new learning. Any time new information comes into the brain, one of the first things the brain looks for is an existing pattern with which it can connect the new learning. Have you ever been in a situation where the speaker is talking about something for which you have no prior learning? Then you know that you may experience a moment of chaos and confusion while your brain searches for something on which to tie the new information. Many students who lack the prerequisite skills to achieve go through this daily. The frustration for some does not end because there is no prior knowledge with which to connect the learning. According to a meta-analysis study by Marzano (1998), one of the most powerful ways to help our students is to provide a connection between the new learning and something they already know. This is much more than simply saying, "Last week we talked about . . . this week we will talk about. . . ." In the PBS series, *Good Morning Miss Toliver*, Kay Toliver relates fractions to pizza because they are always sliced in fractional parts. She knows that her students love to eat, and that they like pizza. It may have surprised her inner-city students to learn that the fractional parts vary widely and that buying a slice of pizza for two dollars is only a bargain if the fraction is large enough. Thus the beginning of every lesson should involve helping students make connections between old knowledge and new knowledge. You may ask students to keep learning logs in which you ask them a question prior to the learning. For example, for a lesson on hunger, you might ask them to describe a time when they were really hungry. You might ask questions like: What was your mood? Were you interested in anything but getting something to eat? Would this have been a good time for you to do your math? In this case, you are building empathy because most students have not been really hungry in the way that starving populations experience. When studying an event in history, you might want to bring in pictures, music, smells, and tastes of the time.
- Compare and contrast is another way to introduce a concept, by showing examples and non-examples. You might compare and

contrast literary styles, points of view, mathematical concepts, or other concepts to show students the attributes of the subject you are discussing.

- Organizing the information helps students to create patterns for memory. Allen (2007) found that, "the most researched and validated studies are those focusing on students' organizing information such as those of Simpson and Nist (2000)" (p. 18).

Activating Prior Knowledge

When taught and used appropriately in the classroom, *activating prior knowledge* has an *effect size* of 1.66 (Darling, 1999), which means it can make as much as 45 percentile gains in achievement. For example, the first step in teaching vocabulary is to identify what the students already know about the vocabulary words. Dale (1965) first identified what it means to truly know a word. He used four levels of understanding to determine if vocabulary has meaning to the learner. Using Dale's four questions, we might use a chart like the one in Figure 3.3 to determine how much prior experience our students have had with the vocabulary. It will give you an idea about which vocabulary words most of the students already know and the words for which they have misconceptions.

Figure 3.3 Vocabulary model

Word or Words	Never Heard the Word Before	Heard It, Don't Know What It Means	Recognize It in Context and Know It Is Related to . . .	Know the Word and Can Use It Appropriately. Here Is My Proof . . .
Symmetry			Lines	
Equal to				The same as
Adjacent		x		

In the example, the student indicated that he knows that symmetry is related to lines, but he doesn't know the definition. He thinks that "equal to" means something is the same as something else, and he has heard the word "adjacent" but does not know its definition. This is critical when working with English language learners and with students from poverty. When we work from an abundance model rather than a deficit model in working with diverse learners, we honor the culture and methods of learning from their backgrounds.

We value the experiences they bring to the classroom rather than dwelling on deficits (Williams, 1996). While middle-class America often learns in linear contexts such as lists or bullets, students from other cultures may learn better from storytelling or from demonstrating the knowledge. By checking for prior learning, we are more likely to get a true picture of what students already know rather than from simply asking questions orally.

When we introduce new knowledge to our students, their brains automatically search for what they already know to connect to the new knowledge. If we can help them smooth that transition, we will be helping them to "grab onto" the new information with less frustration. Have you ever read a page of text or listened to a lecture, really paid attention, but had no idea what the information meant? You probably did not have enough prior knowledge of the topic to be able to "grab onto" the new information and have it make sense to your brain.

Knowledge must make sense to the brain before we will believe that we know and understand it (Jensen, 1996). This is one of the reasons why so much is said about modalities and learning. Visual learners may not know and understand the information until they see it visually or see how it works, as in mathematics. Kinesthetic learners (many urban learners are kinesthetic) need to do something with the learning. Auditory learners not only need to hear the learning but require the opportunity to either review it with others orally or with themselves (Jensen, 1996).

Using Semantic Mapping

Semantic mapping is one of the most effective ways to teach vocabulary. Using this tool has an effect size of 42 percentile (Darling, 1999). Allen (2007) defines semantic mapping, based on the work of Stahl and Clark (1987) and Heimlich and Pittelman (1986) as "a teacher-directed study of a word or concept in relation to other related words and ideas" (p. 17). To teach the concept, teachers may use graphic organizers or maps to help students visualize their thinking. A mind map is a way for teachers to demonstrate semantic mapping.

Another valuable type of map is the *attribute wheel*. An attribute wheel is a great tool if you want students to not only know the definitions of genres such as fantasy, tall tale, and myth, but also to know why a tall tale is not the same as a fantasy or myth.

An attribute wheel is an example of semantic mapping that helps the students use what they already know and build on that knowledge to gain understanding. Let's look at a typical benchmark for reading found in all of the states' standards and see how an attribute wheel makes the learning more powerful.

3.1 Identify the forms of fiction and describe the major characteristics of each form. Know the defining characteristics of various genres (i.e., fiction, nonfiction, myths, poems, fantasies, biographies, science fiction, autobiographies, tall tales, supernatural tales).

Like many benchmarks that we see across curriculum areas, this benchmark asks students to know (declarative) the defining characteristics. Defining characteristics are the essential elements that make something what it is. Attribute wheels are an effective way to teach this skill. The following steps (heuristics) will help you as you teach this process.

1. Provide a simple definition of attribute to your students, and explain how you will be using the attribute wheel.

2. Provide students with an attribute wheel frame.

3. Ask them to place what they already know on the spokes of the wheel.

4. Discuss the attributes they have listed, being sure to clarify any misconceptions.

5. Together, add other attributes until you have enough attributes that define the word well.

Figure 3.4 demonstrates an attribute wheel for a tall tale. Using graphic organizers to help students understand vocabulary has a high effect size on student learning. The effect size for using semantic maps such as an attribute wheel to teach vocabulary is 2.25 for a gain of 49 percentile points in achievement (Darling, 1999).

Benchmarks often call for students to be able to compare or contrast people, events, things, concepts, and so on. Elementary level students are often asked to compare or contrast; while middle and high school level students may be asked to *both* compare and contrast. Once students prepare an attribute wheel, compare and contrast become easier.

Figure 3.5 shows a model for teaching students to take the information from their attribute wheels to compare a myth and a tall tale. Sometimes students, particularly at the secondary level, must be able to contrast these same things. When students contrast two things they must first decide most important attributes to determine how the two differ. In this case, we have chosen to look at the main characters, the purpose of the writing, and how the two genres originated. These are critical attributes that make them different. Figure 3.6 shows the results of the contrasting differences.

In the described benchmark, students were asked to compare and contrast the attributes of several genres. Figure 3.7 is a good model to use when you want to contrast several things at the same time.

Figure 3.4 Attribute wheel

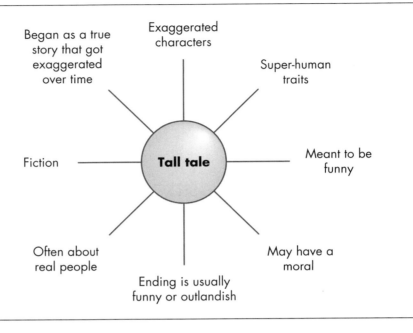

Figure 3.5 Comparison chart: Compare two things, people, events, concepts

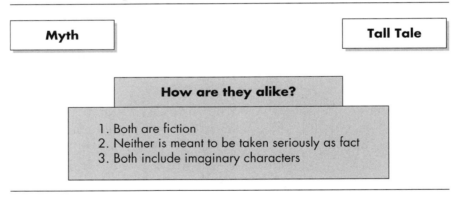

Figure 3.6 Contrast chart: How are they different?

Myth	Different in Regard to	Tall Tale
Imagery, ideal human characteristics	Main character	Human characteristics that are exaggerated
To teach lessons and provide imagery	Purpose	For humor and to test the imagination
Written as a myth	Origin	Started as a story about a real person; became exaggerated with the telling

Figure 3.7   Contrasting in multiples

Tall Tale	Fantasy	Attributes	Fable	Science Fiction
		Main character		
		Purpose		
		Setting		
		Ending		

Down the center column (of Figure 3.7), place the critical attribute categories that you will need to examine to determine how they differ. Across the top, place as many different items as needed to contrast.

Storing Declarative Information

Declarative (semantic) information must have a connector in order to help the brain remember. Some connectors that you might use include:

- Visual representations: These may be actual pictures or concrete objects, or they may be imaginary as you guide students through the thought processes to visualize your discussion. (Note: Students with limited English or students from poverty may not have the language skills to visualize what you are saying.)
- Mnemonic devices: These are peg words, symbols, or cues such as H(uron), O(ntario), M(ichigan), E(rie), S(uperior) (HOMES) for the five Great Lakes.
- Connectors: This involves color coding units or changing the seating arrangement of the classroom before a new unit.

Providing the attribute wheel for the words you are defining helps the brain to store the information more efficiently because the wheel provides a context for the learning. Contextual learning is stored in the episodic pathway of the brain, a much more efficient pathway for retrieval than the semantic memory system where facts are usually stored.

Teaching Vocabulary

Teaching vocabulary is critical if students are to understand and master benchmarks. Most of us learned vocabulary using the "hurt" method. We looked up definitions that often made no sense to us, wrote them down, and memorized them for the test on Friday. Unless we used the words often, we promptly forgot them. This is no longer acceptable in this age of standards and global competition. We want students to learn vocabulary for life, not just for a test. But, how can we do this?

Step 1: Provide background knowledge (Marzano, Pickering, & Pollock, 2001).

We want to know what students already know about the vocabulary, and we want to correct misconceptions before they get put into long-term memory. First, provide students with a table or other visual to help create a pattern and advance organizer for the learning. Then, provide students with the word or words on a graphic organizer and ask them to tell you what they already know about the words. If they do not know the word or have never heard of it, ask them to put that on their graph.

Figure 3.8 shows a sample graph that might be used for students in Grades 2–12.

Step 2: Provide a simple explanation with examples; use visuals when appropriate.

You will want to provide your students with a working definition of the word or words being studied. You will also want to clear up any misunderstandings that your students may have about the word or words. It is also important to provide examples and non-examples of the meaning of the word or words. Pictures, graphs, and models can prove critical, especially if you have English language learners. Remember that they may not have the background knowledge to understand a verbal definition. Some examples of ways to provide a brief explanation and visual of the new words include

- Use direct experiences that provide examples.
- Use a story format.
- Use images.
- Let students teach the term.
- Use current events.
- Describe your mental picture.
- Find or create pictures of the term.
- Use something that students already have some knowledge about. For example you might say, "Look at your milk container and you will see the word pasteurized. That word means that the milk was heated to kill the bacteria that could make you sick. Louis Pasteur, a man from France, invented the process to make milk safe to drink in the 1800s. That process was then named after him."

Marzano, Pickering, and Pollock's (2001) studies indicate that students learn at a higher rate if they are provided no more than seven vocabulary words at a time for secondary and considerably less for younger students. If your unit of study has 20 words that are essential to the learning, break them up into manageable chunks to be taught daily.

Step 3: Teach the word or words in context.

The words need to have significance to the learner. When students ask, "Why am I learning this?" they have a real reason for

Figure 3.8   Blank terminology chart

Word	What I Know	My Definition	Symbol

doing so. Students are constantly bombarded with new information that leads the brain to ask: "If I don't need this, I am going to toss it." The brain literally does this. Brain researchers say that we take in about 98 percent of our new knowledge through our senses—smell, taste, hearing, seeing, feeling—and that the brain discards about 99 percent of all incoming information (Jensen, 1996). The good news is that this filtering system keeps us from becoming phobic; the bad news is that our students' brains often toss out information that we wish they had processed and sent to long-term memory. By teaching in context, we give meaning to the vocabulary, and we provide a connector so that it can be stored and retrieved more efficiently. Teaching vocabulary in context can make as much as 41 percentile point gains in achievement (Darling, 1999).

Step 4: Ask students to write the definition(s) in their own words. Figure 3.9 shows the same graph but with the new definitions written by the student.

Why do we ask students to write the definitions in their own words rather than ask them to copy the definition from the text or dictionary? We remember the things that have personal meaning to us. When students put the definitions into their own words, they are more likely to remember them, and we are more likely to have more

Figure 3.9   Terminology chart with students' definitions: Step 4

Vocabulary	What You Know		
Myth	Not true		
Fable	Not sure		
Tall tale	Story about a big person		

than surface knowledge of them. Think about all the things in school that you memorized for a test and then promptly forgot afterward. Think about the factual pieces of information that you memorized at a surface level but could not explain today. Having verbal/vocabulary skills is the mark of an educated person; we want our students to be highly literate in this 21st century global world (Pink, 2005).

Step 5: Graphic representation of the word or words.

The last step is crucial if you work with English language learners or with students who are highly visual learners. This is quickly becoming a trait of most of our learners as more digital students enter our classrooms. Digital learners prefer to see information first; they need visuals for information to make sense to them. It is how their brains have been wired since birth. We come into this world with about 50 percent of our neurological wiring in place; the other 50 percent takes place after birth and is affected by our environment. For example, our fathers' generation listened to the radio, read books, sat at the dinner table together each night, and talked to each other (yes, they actually did that). So it was easy for our fathers to sit in a classroom, listen, and take notes. Their brains were wired to receive information that way. Our students' brains are wired to take in a multimedia world, to parallel process, and to see the information as well as hear it.

Graphic representations assist students in "dual-encoding" of information for storage by representing knowledge and elaborating on it. Pictographic representations of information are used to gain a better understanding. Drawings that use symbols or symbolic pictures, colors, and linguistic or nonlinguistic forms to depict important information are examples of graphic representations. If the graphic orders the information, gives it a pattern, or shows interrelationships amongst the parts, it may be considered a *graphic organizer*. Common patterns into which most information can be organized include descriptive patterns, time-sequence patterns, process/cause-effect patterns, episode patterns, generalization/principle patterns, and concept patterns (Marzano, Pickering, and Pollock, 2001). Graphic representations and graphic organizers engage students in kinesthetic activity. This activity associated with specific knowledge generates a mental image of the knowledge in the mind of the learner, helping to embed it into long-term memory. Allowing students to demonstrate their understanding of concepts, story sequences, problem solving, or content comprehension through graphic representations can create authentic assessments that are ideal for strong visual learners. Urban learners tend to have kinesthetic and visual strengths. Therefore, graphic representation or organizers are a very effective tool to use with these populations.

Figure 3.10 shows the same graph with a drawing to help the student remember the meaning of the new word. Recall for highly visual students will be based on remembering the graphic first, then the definition. We have just provided the brain (that is in overload from having to recall so much) with a hook.

Figure 3.10 Completed terminology chart with graphic: Step 5

Vocabulary	What You Know	Definition	Symbol
Myth	Not true	A fictional story that explains a practice or occurrence based on the activities of gods or heroes	
Fable	Not sure	A fictional story that teaches a moral or makes its point using animals that speak like humans	
Tall tale	Story about a big person	A fictional story about a real person who became exaggerated over time giving the character super-human characteristics	**T**

DIVERSE LEARNERS AND VOCABULARY

Educators must take diverse learners into consideration when developing lessons and assessments. The instructional approach as well as the assessment format may vary, while still holding students accountable for learning the content and performance standards that are expected of all students. Vocabulary development is crucial when new concepts are introduced. We often take for granted that students have the basic vocabulary that can be transferred to the new topic, but this is a mistake when you are teaching diverse learners. These students need extra time and attention devoted to them in order to learn the oral and written vocabulary and prior knowledge before they can learn new information. To learn words, students need the words to be meaningful, they need multiple exposures to the words, and they need opportunities to use the words. It's also important to note that English language learners will acquire vocabulary on their own, through interaction with other students and adults in and out of school and through reading. A tip: Incorporate graphic representations of vocabulary as much as possible using a variety of methods, ranging from pictorial representations to various graphic organizers. Pre-teach and re-teach vocabulary. When you help students with key vocabulary ahead of time, it will enhance their ability to engage in the reading or lesson that follows (Carroll, 2007).

BUILDING BACKGROUND KNOWLEDGE FOR CULTURALLY DIVERSE STUDENTS

As educators, we are aware that student prior knowledge affects the understanding of new knowledge and concepts. It's important to keep in mind the fact that culturally diverse students and students of poverty come with background knowledge that is likely to be different from what most mainstream curricula assume that students have. How then do we work with background knowledge in the classroom? The first step is to recognize and value the background knowledge that diverse learners may have. Find ways to learn about the knowledge they bring with them (Carroll, 2007). Some other suggestions include

- Provide writing opportunities that allow students to work from their own background and experiences, particularly when they are able to choose their own topics.
- Build background knowledge in all areas of the curriculum. Information that students learn in science, social studies, math, and so forth will help them to increase their vocabulary and to communicate more effectively.
- Use thematic teaching as much as possible. All the benefits of using thematic teaching to develop vocabulary also apply to background knowledge. If you are actually working with plants (or fish, or fabric, or whatever), you will bring that knowledge to reading about the same topic or reading stories that are related to the topic.
- Build specific background knowledge needed for reading particular texts. Look carefully at the texts before you use them for instruction, and figure out what kinds of things students will need to know in order to be able to read them. Spend time building the necessary knowledge prior to reading.
- Allow students to bring some of their own background knowledge into the arena as you assess their knowledge of standards (Carroll, 2007).

PROVIDING VISUAL REPRESENTATIONS AND KINESTHETIC OPPORTUNITIES

Research tells us that culturally diverse students and students of poverty tend to have strengths in visual and kinesthetic intelligences. Visual representations include the use of real objects, pictures, videos, maps, charts, diagrams, graphic organizers, and so forth. Kinesthetic activities allow for fine motor and gross motor skills to come into action.

How can we use these to help our diverse learners?

- Whenever possible, include experiences with real materials.
- When teaching or assessing the food groups, bring food into class.
- If you are teaching or assessing plants, grow some.
- When the real thing can't be brought to class, try simulations or videos.
- If you are learning about weather conditions or natural phenomena, make a simulation. There are videos available on almost every topic.
- Use pictures to help students understand text and learn new vocabulary.
- Use diagrams, especially when reading nonfiction texts—they are often included as part of the text because they are so helpful.
- Create graphic organizers for various purposes. You can create organizers to show the structures of texts and include important ideas or events. You can also create organizers to show information that you're teaching in particular content areas. Graphic organizers are a powerful tool in teaching and assessing vocabulary. Students can use graphic organizers in writing as part of their prewriting activity. While numerous graphic organizers are commercially available, you can also make your own.
- Encourage students to make pictorial representations of the texts they have read, the things they have learned, or their ideas for writing.
- Allow assessment opportunities that include skits, performances, working with clay, dance, and other forms of kinesthetic activity.
- In other words, make the learning active and include all of the senses when possible (Carroll, 2007).

FINDING AND USING RESEARCH ON BEST PRACTICES

If only we were dealing with a product without many variables, then knowing how to build it would be much easier. We know as educators that there is a huge difference between educating children with all of their diversity and creating a product like widgets. One of the best ways that we have to determine whether an instructional practice is sound is to look at it in terms of current brain research and the research on instruction. A meta-analysis is a study of the studies. Good meta-analyses are not based on one or two studies but on many studies and on a diversity of learners. We all have been in those workshops where the presenter says, "I know this works because it worked in my school." We now know that just because a teaching process worked in one instance does not make it a "best practice." Best practices are born over time and with many trials. Look for research that provides an impact on learning or effect size—i.e., if I use this practice, what is the "effect" or "impact" on student learning?

FORMATIVE AND SUMMATIVE CLASSROOM ASSESSMENTS OF DECLARATIVE KNOWLEDGE

We have talked a great deal about how declarative knowledge is assessed on high-stakes tests and the importance of vocabulary in order to master the benchmarks. In the classroom, as we align our lessons to the standards and benchmarks, how do we assess declarative knowledge in general?

Declarative knowledge is assessed by asking students to provide examples and to identify relationships and distinctions. Appropriate *testing formats* to assess declarative knowledge might include

- Completing a cause and effect chart
- Showing examples and non-examples of a concept or idea
- Writing an essay to show understanding of concepts, principles, or ideas
- Completing a selected response test (i.e., matching, multiple choice, true/false)
- Completing or creating a graphic representation that demonstrates understanding of the objective

Figure 3.11 is an example of how declarative knowledge might be assessed and ways not to assess declarative knowledge.

Let's look back at the declarative standards and the examples in Figure 3.11. Can you see a difference in the two kinds of assessments for each standard? Since we are assessing declarative knowledge in each of these standards, we should only assess student understanding of the "what"—*what* the animal characteristics are, *what* the six traits of

Figure 3.11   Assessing declarative knowledge

Declarative Knowledge Standards	Example Assessments
Understands that animals have characteristics that help them adapt to their environment	Students fill in a graphic organizer that lists three animals with the characteristics that help them to adapt to the environment
Knows the causes and effects of the American Revolution	Students create a journal entry where the left page of the journal lists at least five causes and the right page lists five effects of the American Revolution
Knows the six traits of writing	Students demonstrate that they know the six traits of writing in a fill in the blank or selected response test
Knows the attributes that are necessary for plant life to thrive	Students draw an illustration of a plant and include the necessary components (i.e., oxygen, sunlight, water)
Identifies even and odd numbers on a number line	Students color all even numbers blue and all odd numbers red in a teacher-made test

SOURCE: Doty, 2007. Reprinted with permission from Learning Bridges.

writing are, or *what* odd and even numbers are. The non-examples all ask students to use processes with that information. Having students write a journal entry from a British and American point of view is a wonderful lesson plan idea, but it is not appropriate to assess whether or not students understand the basic causes and effects of the American Revolution. If your standard had said, "Compare British and American viewpoints regarding the causes of the American Revolution," then you would have an appropriate assessment.

IN SUMMARY

In this chapter we have added critical pieces for teaching and assessing declarative knowledge. In the studies from Learning Bridges on the impact of training teachers to teach vocabulary in preparation for high-stakes testing, the overall student gain was 20 percentile in achievement. Think about your classroom today. What if the average test score in your classroom could be raised by 20 percentile? For many students that is the difference between failure and success.

We have added to the model in Figure 3.12 to include the teaching practices needed to teach the declarative benchmarks as well as the effect size of each.

Figure 3.12 The model: Step 3

Benchmark	Type of Knowledge D=declarative P=procedural B=both	Level of Understanding K=knowledge C=comprehension Ap=application An=analysis S=synthesis E=evaluation	Essential Vocabulary	Instructional Practice	Effect Size
Knows basic geometric language for describing and naming shapes (e.g., square, triangle, cube, circle, sphere).	D	K	Shapes Square Triangle Cube Circle Sphere	Activating prior knowledge Semantic maps to teach vocabulary	ES = 1.66 (45 percentile) ES = 2.25 (48 percentile)
Understands the basic properties and similarities and differences in shapes.	D	An	Similarity Difference Properties Corner Round Point Two or three dimensionality Symmetry	Attribute wheels or other graphic organizers to teach properties Compare and contrast charts	ES = 2.25 (48 percentile) ES = 1.32 (41 percentile)

4

Teaching and Assessing Procedural Knowledge Standards

The classroom teacher is the most appropriate educator to collect assessment data regarding student performance on standards and benchmarks. That is not to say that external assessments designed at the national, state, or district levels should not be used. Indeed, they provide useful information. However, they should be considered supplemental *[emphasis mine] to the assessment information produced at the classroom level by teachers. (p. 109)*

—Robert Marzano and
John Kendall, *Designing Standards-Based Districts, Schools, and Classrooms* (1996)

In the previous chapter, we discussed how to identify declarative knowledge standards, how to teach to that type of standard, and how best to assess children's learning of declarative knowledge standards.

In this chapter, we will

1. Identify procedural knowledge standards

2. Examine highly effective, research-based instructional strategies appropriate for procedural knowledge standards

3. Explore classroom assessment options that provide meaningful information on student learning of procedural knowledge standards

IDENTIFYING PROCEDURAL KNOWLEDGE STANDARDS AND BENCHMARKS

As we have said, procedural knowledge refers to what we want our students to be able to do as a result of the learning. The procedural knowledge standards and benchmarks will usually have verbs that identify the process, the skill, the algorithm, the strategy, or the macro-processes that indicate that students need to demonstrate something.

Examine the following benchmarks drawn from different states. Note the performance that is required.

From California: Grade 3 Language Arts
Read aloud narrative and expository text fluently and accurately and with appropriate pacing, intonation, and expression.

From California: Grades 9–12 Algebra 1
Students solve equations and inequalities involving absolute values.

From New York: Grades 5–8 Language Arts
Assess the **quality** of texts and presentations, using criteria related to the genre, the subject area, and purpose (e.g., using the criteria of accuracy, objectivity, comprehensiveness, and understanding of the game to evaluate a sports editorial).

From Florida: Grades 9–12 Data Analysis and Probability
Calculates measures of central tendency (mean, median, and mode) and dispersion (range, standard deviation, and variance) for complex sets of data, and determines the most meaningful measure to describe the data.

In all of the examples, students are required to DO something to demonstrate their procedural knowledge. This is different than just "knowing" or "understanding" information (which is declarative knowledge).

TEACHING PROCEDURAL KNOWLEDGE STANDARDS AND BENCHMARKS

Procedural knowledge must pass through several processes in order for the learning to be a part of long-term memory. These include:

Constructing Mental Models

Just as the first phase of learning a skill or process is developing a rough model of the steps involved, so learning procedural knowledge is a matter of learning and understanding the steps involved in demonstrating the process. Some ways to do this include

1. Teach students to talk through the process by demonstrating how you talk yourself through processes. For example, a French teacher might think aloud as she goes through the process of breaking a sentence into its grammatical parts. Sometimes called *think aloud* or *verbalization,* this strategy can make as much as 46 percentile point gains in achievement (Darling, 1999).

2. Provide a written set of steps. For example, a teacher provides students with the written steps for writing a limerick and then demonstrates each step as she reads it. A set of steps outlining the process is sometimes called an *algorithm.*

3. Provide models or examples for students. Teach students to use flow charts or other visual models. For example for a unit on weather, the teacher might have the students work in small groups to make a flow chart of the steps that take place in a weather pattern.

Heuristics are the general rules, tactics, and strategies (as opposed to a set of rigid steps) for implementing processes such as decision making, experimental inquiry, problem solving, investigation, reading, speaking, and listening. Students apply and practice the general rules, tactics, and strategies, paying attention to how they might be improved. When teachers provide students with a guide that outlines the components and subcomponents of a process, they are providing students with a heuristic. For the purpose of this book, we define heuristics as:

> A loosely organized set of skills, tactics, or strategies represented verbally, linguistically, or graphically, and used as a guide to facilitate the performance of an overall process such as writing, speaking, reading, listening, problem solving, decision making, inquiry, and investigation. (Darling, 1999)

Using heuristics with procedural knowledge benchmarks can increase achievement by as much as 38 percentile points (Darling,

1999). The following example (see Figure 4.1) comes from *Simple Heuristics That Make Us Smart,* by Gerd Gigerenzer, Peter Todd, and the ABC Research Group.

A simple *decision tree* for classifying heart attack victims as high or low-risk patients is a good example of a simple heuristic used to accomplish a very complex procedure. Rather than measuring and considering 19 predictors, a doctor can answer at most three questions to determine the patient's risk.

4. Teach students to mentally rehearse the steps involved in a process. For example, a physical education teacher might ask students to rehearse the process of shooting a basket before they actually try it with a basketball.

5. Connect the new skill to a skill they already know how to do.

Figure 4.1 Decision tree heuristic

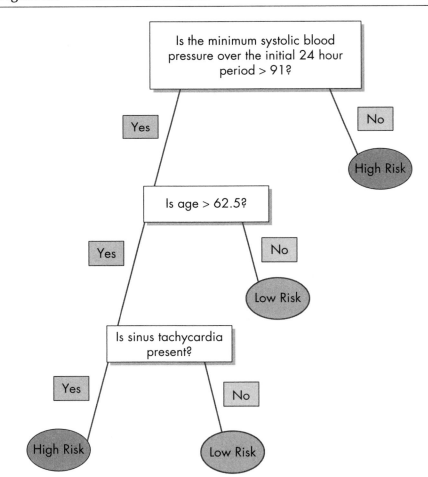

SOURCE: Nei, 2001. Reprinted with permission from Learning Bridges.

Shaping

Constructing an initial mental model for a new skill or process is just the first step in learning procedural knowledge. Once you actually begin to use the skill or process, you'll probably alter your initial model. You'll start to find out what works and what doesn't work and, in response, you'll modify your approach, adding some things and dropping others. This is called shaping. For example, after you constructed an initial model for performing long division, you began to discover some shortcuts and tricks that made the process work better for you (Marzano, 1992).

Some ways that we help students shape the procedural knowledge include

1. Demonstrate and provide practice in the skill or process. As a teacher, it is important that you provide general rules or heuristics about how to do a new process and also provide adequate opportunities for students to practice the learning before you assess. For example, an assessment of procedural knowledge might include asking students to write an essay to show their understanding of concepts, principles, or ideas. An emphasis on quality writing would be an example of procedural knowledge and should include a rubric such as the one shown in Figure 3.2. When we provide this kind of rubric up front before the essays are written, we provide our students with the scaffolding they need to be successful. This is critical when teaching new concepts, just as providing quite a bit of scaffolding in the beginning of a building project is critical to the strength of the structure. There was a time when we would tell our students, "We want you to do this at a quality level!" Unfortunately we found out that what we thought was a quality product and what our students thought was quality was not necessarily the same thing. Just by adding this type of rubric to an assignment raised the level of work of our students tremendously. We think students would do higher quality work if they knew what it looked like. Using a matrix (as shown in Figure 4.2) takes the guesswork out of the equation. In this matrix example, students are asked to write a persuasive essay. The component parts of the essay are found in the left-hand column, while the essential elements for each of the parts are located on the far right-hand side. The center portion shows the number of points earned. Not all parts of the essay are equal in value, hence the center portion.

2. Point out possible pitfalls or common errors that people make when executing the process. For example, a teacher showing

Figure 4.2   Rubric example

Persuasive Essay—Written

Parts (Essentials)	Points	Attributes (Qualities)
Thesis statement		❑ Clear position taken ❑ Logical
Introduction		❑ Attention grabbing ❑ Thesis statement—last sentence
Voice		❑ Targets intended audience
Reasons		❑ Three reasons clearly stated in topic sentence(s) ❑ Emotion/logic-based
Support/elaboration		❑ Transition statements as links ❑ Supported with examples/other elaboration techniques ❑ Clinchers
Conclusions		❑ Restates position statement ❑ Reestablishes reasons ❑ Includes call to action

students the steps involved in reading a contour map tells them that it is easy to misinterpret the altitudes for each contour layer and to make incorrect assumptions about specific types of contours.

3. Provide a variety of situations in which students can use a specific skill or process. For example, a writing teacher demonstrates how she changes the decisions she makes during the editing process based on the audience for whom she writes. She then has students edit a single essay for two different audiences and compare the results.

Automaticity

The final aspect of learning a new skill or process is doing something to the point where you can do it without conscious thought or automaticity. Here are some guidelines:

1. Provide adequate opportunities for practice. Help students self-assess the amount of practice they need and their speed and accuracy.

2. Have students keep a chart of their progress and to self-assess their work.

3. Provide opportunities for metacognition for students to think about what they learned and how they learned it.

4. Provide students with a rubric with which they can self-assess their work. A rubric provides descriptors for each level of performance.

HOW DO WE ASSESS PROCEDURAL KNOWLEDGE IN THE CLASSROOM?

Procedural knowledge involves skills and processes. It is organized by steps, strategies, and macroprocesses. Macroprocesses are big processes with interactive components. Procedural knowledge is usually recognized by, "The student will be able to do. . . ." Specific examples include using language, performing problem-solving steps, scientific reasoning, driving a car, using a lawn mower, and making a telephone call. Processes are similar to skills. However, they are much more complex and usually consist of several component parts that may contain subcomponent parts. For example, the process of writing produces a composition and involves the component parts of pre-writing, writing, revising, and editing.

Figure 4.3   Procedural knowledge assessments

Procedural Knowledge	Sample Assessments
Infers word meaning from context (e.g., surrounding words, examples, restatements, comparisons/contrast)	Students create new sentences using the terminology in a similar context to one that they have read.
Selects the appropriate operation(s) to solve word problems and solve problems with proficiency	On a teacher-made test, or test from a math text, students select the correct operation and solve word problems with 85% accuracy.
Describes the author's use of literary elements (e.g., characterization, setting, plot, theme)	Students write a four- paragraph essay with each paragraph describing one of the literary elements and the students' perception of author use.
Simplifies numerical expressions using the order of operations	Students are given three math problems in which they will correctly simplify numerical expressions using the order of operations.
Connects events and experiences in literature with experiences in own lives	Students create a graphic representation that compares events and experiences from literature to events in students' own lives.

SOURCE: Doty, 2000. Reprinted with permission from Learning Bridges.

Procedural knowledge is usually assessed with rubrics that identify how easily, accurately, and automatically the student is able to perform.

Richard Stiggins, in his book *Student-Centered Classroom Assessment* (1994), notes that different types of assessments should be used for different types of benchmarks. For procedural knowledge, he suggests the following:

1. Essay questions

2. Performance tasks/portfolio

3. Teacher observation

4. Student self-assessment

Essay questions can effectively be used for procedural knowledge when we ask students to critique or explain a procedure.

Here's an example from the Center for Research on Evaluation, Standards, and Student Testing (CRESST) chemistry test (Baker, Aschbacher, Niemi, & Sato, 1992):

> Imagine you are taking a chemistry class with a teacher who has just given the demonstration of chemical analysis you read about earlier.
>
> Since the start of the year, your class has been studying the principles and procedures used in chemical analysis. One of your friends has missed several weeks of class because of illness and is worried about a major exam in chemistry that will be given in two weeks. This friend asks you to explain everything that she will need to know for the exam.
>
> Write an essay in which you explain the most important ideas and principles that your friend should understand. In your essay you should include general concepts and specific facts you know about chemistry, and especially what you know about chemical analysis or identifying unknown substances. You should also explain how the teacher's demonstration illustrates important principles of chemistry.
>
> Be sure to show the relationships among the ideas, facts, and procedures you know. (p. 29)

Performance tasks (sometimes called authentic task) are an excellent way to assess procedural knowledge benchmarks. However they take a great deal of time and effort, so teachers may only want to use them when they are most important. One of the most powerful aspects of performance tasks is that they can be used to assess standards and benchmarks of all types. Evidence is mounting to indicate that the use of performance tasks changes what happens in the classroom. For example, educators have found that performance tasks

- Involve sustained work, often dealing with big ideas and major concepts
- Require students to define the problem and construct a strategy for solving it; encourage group discussion and brainstorming
- Require students to determine what data are needed; collect the data, report, and portray them; and analyze them to discuss sources of error
- Require students to make and explain their assumptions

In addition, performance tasks are grounded in real-world contexts, can be costly, and are not as easy to generalize as originally thought.

An example of a performance task from the Minnesota Profile of Learning (1996) is shown below:

Performance Task: Consumer Smart

Task #1

Area of learning: Managing resources

Topic: Informed consumerism

Benchmark level: Honors middle level

Specific statements from the standard:

What students should know (declarative):

1. Know consumer rights and responsibilities.
2. Know factors which affect consumer decisions.
3. Know how to access information about consumer products.

What students should do (procedural):

1. Describe a variety of personal or household purchases over a period of time.
2. Compare wants, needs, and available resources.
3. Evaluate the impact of the total purchases on the total household budget.

Product:

1. Scenario worksheet
2. General budget worksheet
3. Purchasing record sheet
4. Summary

Central learning:

- Identify and apply criteria to make judgments about a product, situation, or idea.

Task description:

Overview: You have learned about some of the factors that influence what you buy and how you use money. In this task you will pretend to be an adult with a job and different expenses to consider. You will develop a personal budget and goals for how you will spend your money. You will also chart your personal and household purchases over a month-long period, and write a summary of what you have learned about your consumer decisions.

1. Your teacher will have available cards or slips of paper for you to draw from. The "job card" you draw will give you information about your "job" for the next month. It includes the net amount of your monthly income (how much money you have each month after taxes are deducted). Next you will draw an expense card that will identify and give the amounts of a number of fixed monthly expenses. The last card you draw will indicate how many people are in your household and the location of your community. Write all of this information down on your scenario worksheet. (See Figure 4.4: Example 1)

Figure 4.4   Scenario worksheet

Performance Task #1
Consumer Smart
Example 1: Scenario Worksheet

Name: _____ Job: _____

Number of people in household: _____

Location: _____

1. Summarize information about factors that influence consumer spending for transportation. Cite your sources of this information.

2. List the types of transportation that are available to you, along with their approximate monthly costs. (Review the class resources under transportation.)

3. What type of transportation are you going to choose?

   • Is your monthly transportation cost a minor, intermediate, or major expense for you?

   • Explain the three main factors which influenced your transportation choice.

4. Summarize information about factors that influence consumer spending for housing. Cite your sources for this information.

5. List the types of shelter available to you, along with their approximate monthly costs. (Review the class resources under shelter or housing.)

6. What type of shelter are you going to choose?

   • Is your monthly house cost a minor, intermediate, or major expense for you?

   • Explain the three main factors that influenced your choice of shelter.

(Continued)

(Continued)

Your teacher will ask the class to consider products and services that people usually have to pay for in a month and will write them on the board or on a poster. [Your teacher] will ask you to bring some catalogues, newspaper advertisement supplements, and other information that shows prices of apartments, houses, utilities, cars, parking, meals, groceries, clothing, etc. Bring in as much information as you can find on the prices of ordinary goods and services. Create a price display board with this information arranged in categories (such as housing, groceries, and transportation) for classroom use.

2. Your teacher will give you some background information on different factors that influence people's buying decisions, such as income, home type and location, personal preference, cost, quality, environmental considerations, familiarity and availability of products and services, and advertising. You will work in a small group to study one purchasing factor. Your group will research that factor to determine how it influences consumer decisions. Your teacher will have available consumer magazines and other resources for your group. As a group, create a display poster, handout, or transparency to share with the class the most important information you discover about the factor you have studied.

    Finish your scenario sheet by answering the questions about your transportation and shelter, and how different factors might affect your personal spending decision.

3. You need to complete a worksheet to get a general idea for your budget. (See Figure 4.5: Example 2) Use a pencil since you may be changing some figures. On the back of the worksheet, list the purchases you think you will want or need to make over a month-long period. ("Wants" and "needs" are personal decisions. People will define them differently.) List real-life prices for these products or services by checking the price display board, newspapers, asking adults, etc. Then determine the amounts for your different spending categories. (The three spending categories are determined by the percentage of income you are spending. Anything that costs less than one percent of your income is the "minor" spending category, from one to ten percent of your income is the "intermediate" spending category, and over ten percent of your income is the "major" spending category.)

    Now fill in your wants and needs according to their spending category in the space provided on the worksheet. Include the cost next to the product or service.

    Next, determine what your general budget will look like by subtracting your major spending needs from your monthly income. If you have enough money left over, you should subtract your major spending wants. If you find you are over budget, you may have to eliminate some of your wants, or even your needs, from your general budget. Keep them listed on your wants and needs list but indicate (by circling or highlighting) which items you decide to eliminate. You may need to reconsider your shelter and transportation choices. Or you might decide to make some compromises. For example,

Figure 4.5   General budget worksheet

Performance Task #1
Consumer Smart
Example 2: General Budget Worksheet

Determine the amount of money you have available after you have paid your fixed expenses.

Total income: _____

Total fixed expenses: _____

Remainder: _____

Spending Category	Needs	Wants
Minor purchases (less than 1% of income)		
Intermediate purchases (1% to 10% of income)		
Major purchases (more than 10% of income)		

(Continued)

(Continued)

if having a car is very important, you might have to reduce spending in other areas. (Remember to figure in monthly cost for car payments, gas, and insurance.) Or you may decide to look at other options for transportation after initially filling out your general budget, such as ride sharing, biking, and walking.

After subtracting your major expenses, you may want to divide any money you have left over in order to determine how much to spend during each week. You might also consider putting extra money aside for emergencies, since at some point during the month your teacher will ask you to draw a "problem" card.

Keep your budget worksheet available during the month you are working on your purchasing grid.

4. Now that you have some idea of costs for various purchases, and know your major spending categories and how much of your income they will take up, you must create and maintain a month-long record sheet of purchases. Your teacher might ask you to use a particular format. Generally your record sheet must display the following:

- Approximately 30 calendar days
- At least one purchase each day of products and/or services that you need or want
- The cost of each purchase (based on real-life prices)
- Your calculations to show how much money you have left after each day's purchases

To make this as close as possible to an actual, real-life situation, think about the purchases someone in a situation like your scenario might make. You may also include purchases that you actually make if they fit into your budget. For example, if you buy a candy bar, a video game, or rent a movie, record those items and the actual prices you pay for them. To determine what other purchases to record, ask adults what types of things they might need or want to purchase during a given day. You can also get ideas from observing adults, and from advertisements, television programs, and reading. Find the actual prices by checking the classroom display board, other written sources, or by asking adults for information about prices. For your grocery shopping, put the total amount for your groceries on the record, but attach a list that includes each grocery item and its cost.

As you make purchases, be sure that you are aware of the amount of money you have available. Include a realistic variety of both household and personal purchases.

Halfway through the month, your teacher will ask you to draw another card or slip of paper, which will present you with an unexpected financial problem. Your "problem card" will describe the problem, but will not tell you what to do about it. You must use resources to determine what products or services you need in order to resolve the problems. You will need to decide how and where to get what you need and how the costs will affect your budget.

After doing your research and making your decision about how to handle the situation, you will make a brief report to the class in which you describe your decision-making process related to your problem situation. Include the following:

- The information from your scenario (to clarify your personal financial situation)
- How you decided to handle the problem
- All of the factors that you had to consider as you made your decision
- Specify how the problem affected your budgeting and your spending (perhaps you had to borrow money or forego the purchase of other needs or wants, or live with the consequences of putting off resolving the problem until later, or maybe you found an inexpensive way to resolve the problem).

When you have finished recording your purchases, indicate the amount of any money you have left over.

5. In small groups, share and discuss your findings with other students in your class. Consider the following questions for your individual spending and spending patterns as a group:

- What patterns do you notice about the way you spent money?
- How did your purchases of needs and wants affect your budget?
- What motivated you to purchase particular products and services? Be specific.
- Describe how you typically make the decision to purchase products and services.
- How can you tell when you've made a good spending decision? How do you decide whether or not you are satisfied with your purchases?

As a group, record your answers on chart paper. Briefly present your findings and your chart to the entire class.

6. Write a summary of what you have learned, using the following list of questions as a guideline:

- Discuss five factors which you think influence consumer purchasing decisions the most.
- Describe specific examples to show how at least two of those factors affect your spending.
- Describe ways that people address financial needs that arise unexpectedly. Explain ways that unexpected costs affect budgeting.
- List factors that complicate personal and household budgeting.
- Regarding your scenario, if you kept your budget the same each month, what would be your financial status six months from now?
- Would you change anything in your purchase habits as a result of comparing your spending habits to your income? Explain.

Figure 4.6 Checklist for evaluation

Performance Criteria: Checklist for Task #1
Consumer Smart

E = Excellent

S = Satisfactory

N = Needs Improvement

Student	Scenario Worksheet Responses	Teacher
	Identify significant factors that actually influence consumer spending for transportation and housing needs.	
	Incorporate real-life information about adult consumer decision making.	
	Identify actual housing and transportation costs.	
	Realistically portray the relationship between income and spending for housing and transportation.	
	General Budget Worksheet	
	Establishes a budget based on realistic information about personal and household wants, needs, and available resources.	
	Purchasing Record Sheet	
	Clearly displays a month-long record of purchased products and services.	
	Includes a realistic variety of household and personal purchases.	
	Indicates accurate information about costs of products and services.	
	Accurately shows expenditure of resources.	
	Summary	
	Clearly explains significant factors that usually influence consumer-spending decisions.	
	Refers to real-life information to evaluate the impact of total purchases on a household budget.	
	Overall Evaluation	

Notes following performance:

Attach all documents that are appropriate to this performance task.

Teacher observations are another way that teachers can assess procedural knowledge benchmarks. Observations on student behavior that demonstrates learning can be recorded for each student. Primary teachers often do this to record the level of fluency as their students read aloud to them. Although there are a number of devices available to record teachers' observations, a simple daily log will do.

Student self-assessment is a powerful way to measure a student's performance on procedural knowledge because it results in the students setting goals for themselves . Individual learning goals are the heart of the assessment process. Self-assessment can be as simple as a checklist against a specific set of criteria (e.g., the self-assessment in the performance tasks), or it can be more in-depth, such as a student learning log. When students create learning logs, they not only keep a record of their perceptions of their learning but also provide evidence for their self-evaluation. Students can use their learning log as a tool for communicating at student-led conferences. Students can also self-assess their learning of procedural benchmarks if given a good rubric which describes the *levels of performance* (e.g., novice, basic, proficient, or expert) for each *criteria* (e.g., traits of good writing) for the learning task.

IN SUMMARY

In summary, procedural knowledge benchmarks can be identified by the demonstrations required to show learning and accomplishment. We teach procedural knowledge differently than we do declarative knowledge benchmarks. For procedural knowledge benchmarks, we use instructional strategies that help students create mental models, provide heuristics, and shape behavior. We assess procedural benchmarks differently as well. We use essays, performance tasks, portfolios, teacher observations, and student self assessment to measure the degree of proficiency on procedural knowledge benchmarks.

Mapping Lessons to Standards

The three major purposes of public education have remained consistent over many decades. Although different authors may use different terminology, the purposes are (1) to help individuals develop to their fullest potential—physically, emotionally, philosophically, aesthetically, and intellectually; (2) to prepare students for economic self-sufficiency and the world of work, teaching them how to obtain and produce desired goods and services and efficiently manage personal resources; and (3) to instill responsibility for participating in society—maintaining an environment conducive to human survival and functioning effectively for the well-being of the community. (p. 1)

—Arthur Costa, *Developing Minds* (2001)

Virtually every study that has examined the role of the classroom teacher in the process of educating students has come to the same straightforward conclusion: an effective teacher enhances student learning more than any other aspect of schooling that can be controlled. (p. 1)

—Robert Marzano, *Classroom Assessment and Grading That Work* (2006)

In previous chapters we provided graphic organizers along with examples that demonstrate how to unpack standards to determine what students really need to know and be able to do. We describe benchmarks as being either declarative, procedural, or a combination of both. We note that it's important to determine the type of required knowledge because students learn the two types of knowledge differently.

Chapter 1 focused on finding the benchmarks and determining the level of complexity using Bloom's *Taxonomy* (1956).

Chapter 2 examined benchmarks to determine whether they were declarative, procedural, or both. The graphic used in Chapter 1 added another component in our analysis of the benchmarks or indicators.

Chapter 3 revisited declarative benchmarks to determine the most effective ways to teach and assess this type of knowledge in the classroom. In instances where the *effect size* from research was known, we provided it. Thus we added another layer to our graphic to include how we would teach and assess the benchmark.

Chapter 4 repeated the steps in Chapter 3, only this time for procedural benchmarks.

In this chapter, we bring together information from the previous chapters to help you formulate a plan for mapping classroom units, lessons, and assessments to state standards.

When we look at curriculum as a whole, we usually think of it in terms of content, process, and product. In fact, alignment is based on three components: (1) what are we going to teach, (2) how will we teach it, and (3) what will the end results be. To develop and use a mapping structure that ensures students will know and be able to use the standards and benchmarks, we must first look at these three curriculum areas:

1. *Content.* What are we going to teach? What has been determined to be the essential knowledge and skills that must be taught (standards and benchmarks) and then what are the knowledge and skills that have been determined on a local level to be important enough to teach? (local curriculum or enrichment)

2. *Process.* How will we teach the essential and important knowledge and skills? The process includes instructional practices, modalities, differentiation, and scaffolding.

3. *Product.* How will we know that the students know and can use the learning at the appropriate level of understanding for their age, grade level, and subject? Here, students will present this evidence of learning. Products can be anything from verbally answering questions to projects that take weeks to

complete. They may be assessments—formative and summative. Products might be written, auditory, or kinesthetic or combinations of any and all of these.

FIRST THINGS FIRST

Before mapping can take place effectively, it is important that the education staff become familiar with the standards and benchmarks for their grade levels and subject areas. Each state makes those available online through the state education Web sites. If the state in which you teach has benchmarks that are either too vague or too broad to use for lesson planning, a major process in which educators add to those benchmarks for the appropriate grade levels and subjects must take place first. For the purposes of this book, we will make the assumption that the benchmarks are in place so that mapping can be developed and implemented.

It follows, naturally, that once we determine who will teach which benchmarks and when we expect students to show mastery, then we can close the gap between what is taught in the classroom and standards. And once we have closed that gap, we then can close the assessment gap by ensuring that we assess in the classroom those essential knowledge and skills (standards and benchmarks) that make the state assessment just what it is—a summative test over the material taught in the classroom.

LEVELS OF UNDERSTANDING

As we look at mapping lessons to standards, we want to be cognizant of the level of understanding and the level of complexity that is required. We like the facets of understanding developed by Wiggins and McTighe (1998, 2005) and found them easy to work in mapping standards and lessons. Daniel Pink, writing in *A Whole New Mind* (2005), notes that two of these facets of understanding— *empathy* and *story*—are considered imperative as we move from an informational age to a conceptual age. Empathy will be a crucial ability in a global world that is so filled with facts at our fingertips— some true, some not. In the words of Pink:

> The capacity for logical thought is one of the things that make us human. But in a world of ubiquitous information and advanced analytic tools, logic alone won't do. What will distinguish those who thrive will be their ability to understand what makes their fellow woman or man tick, to forge relationships, and to care for others. (p. 66)

The other important attribute that is mentioned by Pink is called *story*. Wiggins and McTighe (1998, 2005) call it *interpretation*. It is the ability to explain, persuade, and interpret information through telling a story. As Pink (2005) puts it:

> When our lives are brimming with information and data, it's not enough to marshal an effective argument. Someone somewhere will inevitably track down a counterpoint to rebut your point. The essence of persuasion, communication, and self-understanding has become the ability also to fashion a compelling narrative. (p. 65)

A father tells the story of how difficult it was as a boy living in poverty to get to school. Without transportation and often without enough food, he managed to get there. His story was told to instill in his children how important education is and to make them more thankful that they can get to school and back easily and with a good breakfast. This is an example of what Pink means when he talks about the use of story.

The following outlines the six facets or levels of understanding of a literate person, along with a brief explanation. We will use these to help formulate essential questions for our students to answer as a result of the learning.

1. *Explanation*—To be able to explain, students must have more than surface knowledge; they must be able to justify, to give details, to be able to prove it, to connect it to other things, to know why, and to know what is implied. Think in terms of who, what, when, where, and why. Verbs associated with explanation include explain, justify, generalize, predict, support, verify, prove, and substantiate. For example:
   - In mathematics, the student not only knows the answer but can prove how he/she arrived at the answer.
   - In science, the student not only knows that water, steam, and ice represent water, but can explain the properties of each.

2. *Interpretation*—In order to demonstrate interpretation, a student must have personal understanding and relevance of the information. These students are able to put information into their own words, to tell it in story form or a format that makes it meaningful. Students are able to demonstrate what something means, why it is important, how it makes sense, and why it is important personally—either to themselves or to others. For example:

- Students use a vocabulary matrix to provide their own interpretation of the vocabulary words as we discussed in Chapter 4.
- Early childhood students make drawings to illustrate a new word, rather than writing the interpretation.

3. *Application*—Students who can use application effectively can apply knowledge to new or different contexts. They can make a connection between learning in the classroom to using that learning in the real world. They are also able to make modifications of the information so that it applies to other situations. For example:
   - A student uses information on estimation to enter a contest to guess the number of marbles in a glass jar.
   - A student uses information on fact and opinion to make a prediction about what is going to happen next in a story.

4. *Perspective*—Students who demonstrate perspective understand point of view. They look at information critically and then are able to see it from others' point of view as well as from their own. They use critical analysis to determine if there is adequate evidence for a conclusion; they look at reasonableness and strengths and weaknesses within the knowledge. They ask, "So what?" For example:
   - A student debates the significance of an event in history.
   - A student looks at and dissects an argument from the point of view of both participants.

5. *Empathy*—A student who can show empathy has the ability to look at someone else's feelings neutrally. The student may not agree with that view but has the ability to look at it and see how the other person came to that conclusion. For example:
   - Using the wonderful book, *Alexander, Who Used to be Rich Last Sunday* (Viorst, 1987), kindergarten children are able to discuss why Alexander makes bad choices with money.
   - Using the book, *Hiroshima* (Hersey, 1985), students are able to discuss World War II from the Japanese point of view.

6. *Self-knowledge*—Students who can demonstrate self-knowledge understand and are able to explain how their heritage affects their thinking, and places where they show prejudice or misunderstanding. They realistically know their strengths and weaknesses. For example:
   - Students are able to correctly self-assess.
   - Students are able to understand why they made a certain decision and to evaluate the effect of that decision.

LEVELS OF COMPLEXITY

As we look at products of learning, we will also look at the level of complexity. In Chapter 1 you were provided with the model for complexity by Benjamin Bloom. We have already mapped the benchmarks to the levels of complexity. A word of warning: Do not assume that as you move up the grade levels in a discipline that each grade level will become more complex. In some instances it does; but not always. For example, remember our benchmark for reading where students were required to know and be able to distinguish between various genres such as tall tale, fable, and so on? For this benchmark, additional genres are added at the next few levels. This does not make the benchmark more complex; it just adds more information to learn. There is a difference between a benchmark being more difficult rather than more complex.

MAPPING THE WAY

Educators who want to map their lessons and units of study to state benchmarks and standards should follow these simple steps to align the content (standards and benchmarks) to the processes and then to assessments.

Step 1: Unit Overview and Plan

Using the format in Figure 5.1, plan your units for the semester or year. Figure 5.1 gives a bird's eye view of the essential knowledge and skills that you will be teaching your students based on benchmarks for your grade span and the decisions that have been made regarding what will be taught at your specific grade level and subject area. This chart will help make sure that all benchmarks for your grade level and subject area are taught and when they are taught. It also will provide you with a list of the vocabulary from the standards that has been taught and when.

Not all benchmarks are conducive to a state test format, but they still can be assessed in the classroom. For example, a typical benchmark in each of the states requires students to be able to read using emphasis at appropriate places. This can be easily assessed in the classroom but would be difficult to test in the primarily multiple-choice format of many current state tests. Not all benchmarks were meant to be assessed on a state exam; some were clearly designated by the required process skills to be assessed in the classroom.

Figure 5.1 shows that the first unit of study in this classroom will be on water. Standard 1 (using the compendium from MCREL,

Figure 5.1   Lesson map

September	October	November
Week 1—Water, water everywhere	**Week 1**—I get a buzz from electricity	**Week 1**—Unit name
Essential question: What is so special about water?	**Essential question:**	**Essential question:**
Performance tasks: • Vocabulary exercise with graph • KNWL (**K**now/ **N**eed to know/ **L**earned/ **H**ow I learned) to tie past experience with new learning • Group research on assigned questions	**Performance tasks:**	**Performance tasks:**
Formative assessment: Rubric for assigned group task	**Formative assessment:**	**Formative assessment:**
Remediation: Provide additional visuals of the vocabulary. Provide visuals of what it is NOT as well.	**Remediation:**	**Remediation:**
Enrichment: Use Bloom's *Taxonomy* for providing the group questions.	**Enrichment:**	**Enrichment:**
Benchmarks: The student is expected to know that water exists in the air in different forms (e.g., in clouds and fog as tiny droplets; in rain, snow, and hail) and changes from one form to another through various processes (e.g., freezing, condensation, precipitation, evaporation). (declarative) D, C	**Benchmarks:**	**Benchmarks:**

(Continued)

Figure 5.1 (Continued)

September	October	November
Vocabulary words: • Forms of water • Freezing • Condensation • Precipitation • Evaporation	**Vocabulary words:**	**Vocabulary words:**
Week 2—Continuation of unit on water **Essential questions:** **Performance tasks:** **Formative assessment:** **Remediation:** **Enrichment:** **Benchmarks:** 1. The student is expected to . . . 2. 3. 4. 5.		
Vocabulary from the benchmarks:		

www.mcrel.org/compendium) under Earth and Space Sciences states, "Understands atmospheric processes and the water cycle." The student will know that

- Water changes from one state to another through various processes
- Water changes from a gas to either a liquid or a solid through precipitation
- Water changes from a liquid to a solid through freezing
- Water changes from a gas to a liquid through condensation
- Water changes from a liquid to a gas through evaporation
- Water exists in the air in different forms
- Fog is made up of tiny droplets of water
- Water can exist in the air as snow
- Water can exist in the air as rain
- Water can exist in the air as hail

Step 2: Unpacking the Unit

Unpacking the unit means moving from the unit with its title, vocabulary, and benchmarks to individual lessons that effectively

1. Teach the objectives based on the benchmarks

2. Determine whether the instructional objectives address *declarative* or *procedural* knowledge and are based on that information

3. Utilize the instructional strategies that make the most difference in student learning

4. Require a student product that demonstrates understanding, such as a performance task, to measure attainment of the benchmark

Use the format in figure 5.1 to determine the component parts of the unit of study. Be sure that you correctly identify declarative and procedural knowledge using the information from Chapter 2.

In Week 1 (of this three-week unit), we will introduce the unit to our students, determine their prior understanding of water, and then create a connection between what they know and what they are about to learn. We begin by telling our students a little about the unit and by providing them with the essential question for Week 1, "What is so special about water?" We will use this question to guide them as we create personal goals for the learning.

Step 3: Determining the Tasks and Performance Tasks

Writing a good performance task requires an understanding of the ABCs (Roy, 1996). Good performance tasks are

- **Authentic**—Ask yourself: "What do people outside of school do with this learning?"
- **Unbiased**—Ask yourself: "Do all my students have an opportunity to be successful doing this task?"
- **Constructivist**—Ask yourself: "Are my students doing the work and making decisions that determine the meaning for their learning?"
- **Developmental**—Ask yourself: "Is this work at the appropriate level for my students?"
- **Embedded**—Ask yourself: "Is this task integrated into my normal classroom activities?"
- **Focused**—Ask yourself: "Are my students demonstrating the learning called for in the benchmark?"
- **Generalizable**—Ask yourself: "If my students do this task, will I be reasonably sure they have the knowledge and skills called for in the benchmark?"
- **High in Rigor**—Ask yourself: "Does this task represent high expectations for student learning?"
- **Interesting**—Ask yourself: "Will my students be interested in doing this task?"

In order for you to write a performance task for your students, you will need to know

1. The concepts and processes (procedural and declarative knowledge) inherent in your state's benchmarks. (You already know how to determine this.)

2. The best practices in instruction for the type of knowledge represented. In *A Different Kind of Classroom: Teaching with Dimensions of Learning* (1992), by Robert Marzano, strategies identified for *declarative knowledge* fall into three categories: constructing meaning, organizing, and storing.

   Constructing meaning—This involves linking old knowledge with new knowledge, making predictions, verifying them, and filling in a lot of unstated information. Examples that teachers can use include
   a. Three-minute pause
   b. Variety of senses
   c. Know, want to know, learned (KWL)

d. Concept attainment

e. Reciprocal teachers (students teach)

f. Before, during, and after

Organizing—This involves helping students put the pieces together. Examples that teachers can use include

a. Pictographs

b. Graphic organizers: descriptive patterns, sequence patterns, process/cause patterns, problem/solution patterns, generalizations patterns, concept patterns

c. Physical models

Storing—This involves consciously storing information in memory. Examples that teachers can use include

a. Imagery

b. Self-talk

c. Symbol substitutes

d. Linking

e. Pegging

f. Mnemonics

The three categories of instructional practices for *procedural knowledge* include constructing models, shaping, and internalizing.

Constructing models—This involves developing a rough model. Examples that teachers can use include

a. Thinking aloud

b. Modeling the process

c. Producing a written set of steps

d. Creating a flow chart

e. Doing a mental rehearsal

Shaping—This involves altering your initial model, so that it becomes meaningful. Examples that teachers can use include

a. Illustrate important variations

b. Ask "What if?"

c. Point out common errors and pitfalls

d. Practice in a variety of situations

Internalizing—This involves attaining automaticity. Examples that teachers can choose from include

a. Practice (first close together and then gradually spaced further apart)

b. Students chart accuracy

c. Fluency, chart speed

3. The criteria for a quality checklist so your students can self-evaluate themselves and you can evaluate them as well. A checklist must do these things:
   a. Differentiate quality work
   b. Align to part of the standard or benchmark
   c. Align to the task description in the performance task
   d. Describe a quality performance/product (not the learner)
   e. Give useful feedback
   f. Include quality indicators that use qualitative language
   g. Use language appropriate to your students
   h. Reflect significant learning

Checklists are NOT "to-do" lists. They are not a simple listing of the parts of the assignment or the activities it takes to complete it. Instead, they define the criteria to use in observing and recording that student learning, and they also become the tools to give students feedback. Two Minnesota educators, Mary Otto and Shelley Roy, created a to-do list and a checklist for getting a clean bedroom. It illustrates the difference in a fun way.

The Clean Bedroom

The *to-do list* might include

_____Vacuum the carpet

_____Dust the furniture

_____Make the bed

_____Pick up clothes off the floor

The *checklist* might include

_____The carpet is free of lint and dirt

_____The furniture is free of any visible dust

_____The comforter and sheets are smooth and free of wrinkles

_____Pillows are placed in the appropriate places

_____All clothing is picked up and put in drawers or hung in closets

Could you complete all of the tasks on the to-do list and still not meet the standard for a clean room? The checklist defines what constitutes quality in a clean room.

For Week 1, we have our students perform three performance tasks that allow us to see their level of understanding. The first task involves creating a vocabulary chart like the one discussed in

Chapter 2. This chart will be an ongoing task as the students will only fill in what they know about the words at this time. We will revisit the chart throughout the unit as we learn the vocabulary in context.

The second type of task is a KNLH chart. (See Figure 5.2 **K**now, **N**eed to know, **L**earned, **H**ow I learned)

Figure 5.2   KNLH chart

Know	**N**eed to know	**L**earned	**H**ow I learned
Water tastes bad sometimes			
The lakes are water			
The ocean water is salty			
Rain is water but we can't drink it			
Fish need water to live			
Water is clear			
Snow is water when it melts			

Categories: 1. 2. 3. 4. 5. 6. 7.

For this task, we ask students to tell us what they know about water. We do this in cooperative learning groups, but it can be done individually. We ask the students to list at least six things they know. Next, in a large group discussion, the students share what they know about water. This is a great opportunity for us to correct misconceptions before they get stored in long-term memory. We then make a classroom list of what they know, using chart paper and markers. Next, we ask students to look at the list and do the following:

- Put a 1 by the things they know have to do with evaporation
- Put a 2 by the things they know have to do with weather
- Put a 3 by the things they know have to do with freezing
- Put a 4 by the things they know have to do with how water affects them personally

- Put a 5 by the things they know they can control (boiling water, freezing popsicles, and so forth)
- Put a 6 by things that have to do with water in the air
- Put a 7 by things they know about water that affect other things besides themselves

We will talk about these things during Week 1 to help build a bridge between what they already know and what they will be learning. The brain likes patterns, and we are creating a pattern up front to help them with the new knowledge.

Next, we remind our students about what we have just discussed and of the essential question (because 87 percent or more of us are visual learners, we put this information up in the room for our students to see). Then, we ask them to write personal goals for the learning such as: "What do you need to know at the end of this unit?"

We will revisit this often during the unit so the students are constantly aware of whether they are meeting their personal goals. Having students set personal goals for their learning and giving them some control over same can make as much as 38 percentile point gains in achievement (Darling, 1999). We will complete the rest of the chart only after we have learned the information in context. We will come back to list the things they have learned and how they learned it—through visuals, research, experiments and so on. It's important to recognize that learning is constantly taking place and how we learn. It helps us on those days when there are no teachers or coaches to help—when we must learn for ourselves.

The third task will be on colored strips of paper and will be based on Bloom's *Taxonomy* (1956). Why? We want to assign questions to groups based on where they are in terms of their learning; on what we know about the level of complexity they can handle without frustration. The best learning environment according to Jensen (1996) is one in which we push the envelope slightly; where students feel some stress but not to the point of frustration. Beware: There is a danger here to make the work too simple, so we are careful to make sure that all groups are challenged. The colors of the strips signal the level of difficulty as we pass them out to the groups. We typically use groups of three; over the years we have found that to be the most manageable. Some examples of questions that we might put on the strips include

1. Why does sweating keep you cool?

2. Why do plants need water?

3. How much water is there in your body?

4. Why do things float?

5. What is hydraulic power?

6. Why do icebergs float in the sea?

7. Who made the first waterwheels?

8. What is hydroelectric power?

The tasks involve activities that you will use to determine the level of understanding and the level of complexity for which students can demonstrate that they know and understand the learning. Use Figure 5.1 (Lesson Map) to list the performance tasks.

Step 4: Providing the Scaffolding

For each performance task, what will students need to be successful? What are the heuristics that are needed in order to show mastery? For example, if students are going to create a mind map, they will need to know the steps for creating a mind map, and they will need to have an opportunity to practice making mind maps. They also need a rubric to show them what is meant by a quality mind map. Go back to Figure 5.1 and list the scaffolding that you will put into place to help students achieve success. For example, before my students define the vocabulary, they will need the following:

1. The chart with a list of the vocabulary they will be using during the week.

2. Directions on how to use the chart. What do they write in the second column, third, and so on? What are the heuristics of the chart? We also have the students keep the charts for all of their units in a notebook so they can review the vocabulary periodically. For elementary and secondary students who have multiple teachers, we suggest they keep the entire vocabulary chart in a notebook with dividers for the different subject areas. Vocabulary words often go across subject areas, so that a word used in science may also show up in mathematics, and so on. Working together, teachers can reinforce this essential vocabulary for all students.

3. Group assignments. We suggest spending some valuable time at the beginning of school helping students know the responsibilities of working with others. If you look back at the SCANS report mentioned in Chapter 1, this report puts working with other people right up there with math and reading on important skills for business and industry. It is an essential skill from Pink as well.

4. Strips of paper with the assignments by levels.

5. A rubric so that students know what is meant by quality work. This is one of the most important pieces that you can add to your classrooms. Many teachers are used to saying to their students, "I want you to do this, and I want you to do it at a quality level." What we have found out, however, was that what teachers consider to be a quality level and what students consider to be a quality level are not always the same. Adding a matrix that tells students exactly what you expect will raise the quality of products in your classrooms greatly.

Step 5: Closing the Gap Between Classroom and State Assessments

An important part of Figure 5.2 is the method in which we will assess the learning on an ongoing basis. As we have already discussed, we use a matrix—which we give students upfront—to determine grades and levels of understanding. Figures 5.3 and 5.4 are generic examples of how to build a matrix for declarative knowledge and how to build a matrix for procedural knowledge.

In addition, we have built in how we will remediate if we determine that the students are not learning at a quality level. If the students do not understand our initial explanation of the vocabulary, we may need to give additional examples, or we may need to give

Figure 5.3 Generic performance levels for procedural benchmarks

Advanced performance	Carries out the major processes and skills inherent in the procedure with relative ease and automaticity
Proficient performance	Carries out the major processes and skills inherent in the procedure without significant error, but not necessarily at an automatic level
Basic performance	Makes a number of errors when carrying out the processes and skills important to the procedure, but still accomplishes the basic purpose of the procedure
Novice performance	Makes so many errors when carrying out the processes and skills important to the procedure that it fails to accomplish its purpose

NOTE: Performance levels for *procedural knowledge* deal with the *ease* and *automaticity* with which skills and processes are carried out.

SOURCE: *Rubrics:* a common convention for referring to *performance levels* on benchmark standards. (Marzano, R. & Kendall, J. (1996). *Designing Standards-Based Districts, Schools, and Classrooms.* Alexandria, VA: ASCD. pp.152–153.) Reprinted with permission of McREL.

Figure 5.4   Generic performance levels for declarative benchmarks

Advanced performance	Demonstrates a thorough understanding of the important information; is able to exemplify that information in detail, and articulates complex relationships and distinctions
Proficient performance	Demonstrates an understanding of the important information; is able to exemplify that information in some detail
Basic performance	Demonstrates an incomplete understanding of the important information, but does not have severe misconceptions
Novice performance	Demonstrates an incomplete understanding of the important information along with severe misconceptions

NOTE: Performance levels for *declarative knowledge* deal with the extent to which examples are provided, relationships and distinctions are articulated, and misconceptions are avoided. A useful convention is to identify the important information along with the key examples, relationships, and distinctions for each level.

nonexamples so that they see the difference. Differentiation plays an important part here. If our groups cannot work together, we need to go back to the structure of cooperative groups and directly teach that. If our groups turn in sloppy work, we want to look first at the rubric that we gave them and ask ourselves if it needs to be more specific or if we need to provide actual examples of past work that was well done.

It's important to remember is that students who do not "get it" usually are either being taught the wrong modality (see, hear, touch, taste, smell), or they do not have the past experience or language skills necessary to make sense of the learning.

IN SUMMARY

When we directly align our lessons with the state benchmarks and standards and when we directly align our formative and summative tests with the state benchmarks and standards, state test scores will go up. If you are not making the progress that you want after making these changes, you may want to look first at whether you are trying to "cover too many benchmarks in one lesson." We know from being in the middle of this research for many years that the key is the proficiency of classroom teachers on the instructional practices that make the most difference in student learning. Notice that we did not say it is based on the proficiency or knowledge of teachers directly. It is not; it is based on the amount and quality of training that has been afforded to teachers on which practice makes the most difference in student learning. For example, if the teachers in your school have not been trained on how to create graphic organizers, how can they be expected to teach students using this technique? Yet when used appropriately, it has a high effect on student learning. If your school has a high number of students from poverty or a high number of English language learners, you will probably not ever meet your goals until you provide teachers with the scaffolding they need to be successful.

We have spent so much money on tests and standards in this country. Now it is time to begin putting resources toward equipping our teachers with the teaching methods that research says makes the most difference in achievement so that all kids can be successful.

Blackline Masters

Benchmark	Type of Knowledge D=declarative P=procedural B=both	Level of Understanding K=knowledge C=comprehension Ap=application An=analysis S=synthesis E=evaluation	Essential Vocabulary	Instructional Practice	Effect Size

September	October	November
Week 1		
Essential Question:		
Performance tasks:		
Formative Assessment:		
Remediation:		
Enrichment:		

References

Allen, J. (2007). *Inside words: Tools for teaching academic vocabulary. Grades 4–12.* Portland, ME: Stenhouse.

Baker, E. L., Aschbacher, P. R., Niemi, D., & Sato, E. (1992). *CRESST performance assessment models: Assessing content area explanations.* Los Angeles: UCLA, National Center for Research on Evaluation, Standards, and Student Testing.

Bloom, B. S. (Ed.). (1956). *Taxonomy of educational objectives. Handbook 1: Cognitive domain.* New York: Longman, Green, & Co.

Carroll, R. (2007). In Classroom Assessment and Data Analysis. [Online course]. Course accessed through www.learningbridges.com

Costa, A. L. (2001). *Developing minds: A resource book for teaching thinking.* (3rd ed.). Alexandria, VA: Association for Supervision and Curriculum Development.

Dale, E. (1965). Vocabulary measurement techniques and major findings. *Elementary English, 42,* 82–88.

Darling, S. K. (1999). *Aligned Instructional Database.* Chandler, AZ: Learning Bridges.

Doty, G. (2007). Classroom Assessment and Data Analysis. [Online course]. Course accessed through www.learningbridges.com

Fisher, D., & Frey, N. (2007). *Checking for understanding: Formative assessment techniques for your classroom.* Alexandria, VA: Association for Supervision and Curriculum Development.

Gigerenzer, G., and Todd, P. M. (1999). *Simple heuristics that make us smart.* New York: Oxford University Press.

Heimlich, J. E., & Pittelman, S. D. (1986). *Semantic mapping: Classroom applications.* Newark, DE: International Reading Association.

Hersey, J. (1985). *Hiroshima.* New York: Alfred A. Knopf.

Jensen, E. (1996). *Completing the puzzle: The brain-compatible approach to learning.* Del Mar, CA: The Brain Store.

Jensen, E. (2003). [Brain Workshop]. Dallas: The Brain Store.

Kendall, J. S., Richardson, A. T., & Ryan, S. E. (2005). *The systematic identification of performance standards.* Aurora, CO: Mid-continent Research for Education and Learning.

Marzano, R. J. (1992). *A different kind of classroom: Teaching with dimensions of learning.* Alexandria, VA: Association for Supervision and Curriculum Development.

Marzano, R. J. (1998). *A theory-based meta-analysis of research on instruction.* Retrieved August 18, 2007, from Mid-continent Research for Education and Learning Web site: www.mcrel.org/compendium/browse.asp

Marzano, R. J. (2004). *Building background knowledge for academic achievement: Research on what works in schools.* Alexandria, VA: Association for Supervision and Curriculum Development.

Marzano, R. J. (2006). *Classroom assessment and grading that work.* Alexandria, VA: Association for Supervision and Curriculum Development.

Marzano, R. J., & Kendall, J. S. (1996). *A comprehensive guide to designing standards-based districts, schools, and classrooms.* Alexandria, VA: Association for Supervision and Curriculum Development.

Marzano, R. J., Kendall, J. S., & Gaddy, B. B. (1999). *Essential knowledge: The debate over what American students should know.* Aurora, CO: Mid-continent for Education and Learning.

Marzano, R. J., Pickering, D. J., & Pollock, J. E. (2001). *Classroom instruction that works: Research-based strategies for increasing student achievement.* Alexandria, VA: Association for Supervision and Curriculum Development.

Minnesota Department of Education. (1996). *Minnesota Profile of Learning.* Retrieved from http://education.state.mn.us/mde/index.html

Nei, K. (2001). Explicit Instruction/Heuristics. [Online course]. Course accessed through www.learningbridges.com

New York State Education Department. (n.d.) *English language arts learning standards.* Retrieved August 18, 2007, from www.highered.nysed.gov/kiap/PCPPU/service_learn/standards/ ela/ela.html

O'Tuel, F. S., & Bullard, R. K. (1993). *Developing higher order thinking in the content areas K-12.* Pacific Grove, CA: Critical Thinking Press and Software.

Pink, D. H. (2005). *A whole new mind: Moving from the information age to the conceptual age.* New York: Riverhead Books.

Ravitch, D. (1995). *National standards in American education: A citizen's guide.* Washington, D.C.: Brookings Institution Press.

Ravitch, D. (2002). *Brookings papers on education policy.* Washington, DC: Brookings Institution.

Roy, S. (1996). *Performance Assessments Training Manual.* St. Cloud, MN: Central Minnesota Educational Service Center.

Simpson, M. L., & Nist, S. L. (2000). An update on strategic learning: It's more than textbook reading strategies. *Journal of Adolescent & Adult Literacy, 43*(6), 528–541.

Squires, D. A. (2004). *Aligning and balancing the standards-based curriculum.* Thousand Oaks, CA: Corwin Press.

Stahl, S. A., & Clark, C. H. (1987). The effects of participatory expectations in classroom discussion on the learning of science vocabulary. *American Educational Research Journal, 24*(4), 541–555.

Stiggins, R. J. (1994). *Student-centered classroom assessment.* New York: Merrill.

Tileston, D. W. (2003). *What every teacher should know about special learners.* Thousand Oaks, CA: Corwin Press.

Viorst, J. (1987). *Alexander, who used to be rich last Sunday.* New York: Aladdin.

Wiggins, G., & McTighe, J. (1998, 2005). *Understanding by design.* Alexandria, VA: Association for Supervision and Curriculum Development.

Williams, B. (1996). What else do we need to know and do? In B. Williams (Ed.), *Closing the achievement gap: A vision for changing beliefs and practices* (2nd ed., pp. 13–24). Alexandria, VA: Association for Supervision and Curriculum Development.

Index

**CORWIN
PRESS**

The Corwin Press logo—a raven striding across an open book—represents the union of courage and learning. Corwin Press is committed to improving education for all learners by publishing books and other professional development resources for those serving the field of PreK–12 education. By providing practical, hands-on materials, Corwin Press continues to carry out the promise of its motto: **"Helping Educators Do Their Work Better."**